# Words & Phrases That Carry Uncommon Meanings



**Dr. A.P. Sharma**
M.A.(Eng.), M.A.(Phil.), PhD.(Edu. & Phil.)

UNICORN BOOKS

*Publisher*
**UNICORN BOOKS**
F-2/16, Ansari Road, Daryaganj, New Delhi-110002
☎ 011-23275434, 23262683, 23250704 • *Fax:* 011-23257790
*E-mail:* info@unicornbooks.in • *Website:* www.unicornbooks.in

**Branch : Mumbai**
23-25, Zaoba Wadi, Thakurdwar, Mumbai-401002
☎ 022-22010941, 022-22053387
*E-mail:* rapidex@bom5.vsnl.net.in

**Showroom :**
★ **PM Publications,** New Delhi
- 10-B, Netaji Subhash Marg, Daryaganj
  New Delhi-110002
- 6686, Khari Baoli, Delhi-110006



ISBN 978-81-7806-095-8
*Words & Phrases that carry Uncommon Meanings*

**Edition:** 2014



***Printed at :*** *Unique Color Carton, Mayapuri, New Delhi-110064*

# Preface

There are a number of common words, phrases or expressions that often carry various meanings and can be used at several occasions, not usually known to a common person. In fact, those who are quite capable of using common words at uncommon occasions, can become good conversationalists. They possess an art of communication that can influence and fascinate people with their verbosity and diction and can win their attention and praise as well. My attempt in this book is to highlight some common connotations that, at times, are used for uncommon situations. If you try to understand their right and correct use, it would not only enhance your capability of conversation but also enrich your word power that may help you at varied occasions.

In this book, I have tried to identify most words or expressions that are often used during everyday talk but many people don't exactly know their right usage. I have also tried to provide appropriate situations to help the reader understand the correct usage and meanings of the expressions so that with a small practice, the connotations could be used properly. More will depend on the reader's desire to learn and update their knowledge in this field.

I have proceeded alphabetically to help the reader look back easily whenever he/she needs to know about a particular expression. Although the selection of phrases and their uses are quite exhaustively dealt with, it is possible that more uses or situations can be there while indulged in a conversation. Despite identifying common words carrying different meanings, altogether different situations have been provided with an appropriate vocabulary in each set of conversation. I have chosen mostly the verb forms of the expressions (idioms), displayed their meanings and knitted them into new sentences to convey their exact uses. Thus, the book has **two** clear **sections**. One deals with the common words that carry different and uncommon meanings. The second part carries the uses of the common words and expressions in different and uncommon situations, projected through dialogues and conversation.

Every piece of conversation is absolutely complete in itself and knitted with a fitting and natural setting. I have tried to use an ingenuous and appropriate language during the conversations keeping in view the background and the scenario contained in the particular situation. Every set of conversation and dialogues is new and presented with a natural zeal projected by the speakers. It often transports the reader to a new scenario, as its setting is absolutely normal and unaffected. As such it is bound to fascinate the reader with the enthusiasm and emotions contained in it.

Yet there is the **third section** which carries some exercises useful to everyone who is interested to improve and enrich his/her spoken or written English. It is also true that the book inadvertently enables the reader to cover a great portion of GMAT or any sort of similar tests held for various entrance positions.

I shall feel really rewarded if the reader is benefited by my humble efforts and develops certain ability to conversing with the people. At this juncture, I would like to implore the reader not to indulge in long dialogues when replying to someone's questions or while making a query to someone. The beauty of English language, so also of any language, lies in delivering short and meaningful expressions. It can happen when the reader is alert, possesses right and good knowledge of the language and can use words correctly. This book has been designed to fulfil that mission only.

August, 2005

**—Dr. A.P. Sharma**
Udaipur

# Contents

# Common Words and Expressions

## Abandon

The simple meaning of abandon is ***to forsake***. The cruel father ***abandoned*** his children to beg. But it has another meaning denoting ***giving oneself up completely***. For example: She abandoned herself to bad ways. He abandoned himself to despair. That means she indulged herself in bad practices. And, he was totally full of despair or he was inclined totally to despair.

## Acknowledge

It is a very common word that is used often by the people during their conversation. The simple meaning it conveys is ***to accept the truth, or reality of***. It means ***confession.*** Most people don't ***acknowledge*** their mistakes. I ***acknowledge*** that I broke the earthen pot. The second use of the term acknowledge, is ***to report about something that one has received.*** For example: We acknowledge with thanks your good services in the company. It is also used ***to convey or to report that one has received the letter or information*** sent to him/her. I ***acknowledge*** with thanks your reply as well as the gifts sent by you.

## Across

A common meaning of across is ***from one side to the other side***. Last night, I walked ***across*** the bridge when it was very dark. Her house is just ***across*** the street. The other meaning of ***across*** is to ***convey some event or happening***. I came ***across*** an old man in the street who was bearing a red turban. It simply means I happened to meet the old man bearing a red turban.

## Acute

The simple meaning of acute is ***sharp or quick or keen.*** People often like to express it when they want ***to convey someone's keenness or sharpness***. Geeta is an acute observer. It simply means that Geeta is a keen observer. But it is also used to express ***some coming crisis or a turning point***. The patient has reached the ***acute*** stage of the disease, the brief period during which the disease is severe and is at *a turning point.*

## Admit

The simple meaning of admit is ***to allow to enter.*** She ***admitted*** the guest ***into*** the house when she identified him properly. Only talented students with high percentage of marks are ***admitted*** in this school. ***Admit*** has yet another meaning too. It means ***to acknowledge, to accept or confess as true or sound convincing.*** The student ***admitted*** his guilt in front of the principal. The use of the term, ***admit*** in this situation is always related to some sort of guilt or mistake or unworthy doing. When some furniture or utensil is broken in a house, often no one would admit to have done it. Thus, ***admit*** simply ***means to accept or to acknowledge***. When two people converse with each other, they often use this term many times. One would say, "I do admit that I said so but I did not do what you are accusing me of."

## Address

It is a very common connotation to denote the ***details of where a person may be found and where letters may be delivered***. "Please write your address correctly so that you don't miss your mail." It is a term that is commonly used during conversation. One may ask you, "What is your home address?" But address has some other meanings too when used in a different context. It denotes ***making a speech*** *and* ***when you use a title***. The Prime Minister will ***address*** the audience now. Please don't ***address*** me as a professor, I am simply a teacher.

## Affair

The simple meaning of affair is ***concern regarding work or business***. For example, I had plenty of affairs today to keep me busy until quite late. But affair has another connotation too. It means ***having an emotional*** (and sexual) ***relationship*** with someone to whom one is not married. For example, "My neighbour is ***having an affair*** with his neighbour's wife."

## After

Sometimes simple words like ***after*** can be used during conversation in two different ways as it gives varied meanings when used in different situations. Its simple meaning is ***following in time.*** I shall see you ***after*** dinner. I shall see you the day ***after*** tomorrow. ***After*** also refers to ***during a time later than***. He will reach here after you leave. Yet ***after*** has another use. It is, ***later in time***. She fell from the roof around midnight and was admitted to the hospital ***after*** two hours. All such uses of ***after*** are little tricky but not quite difficult. Once if the reader gets used to it, it will help him/her enriching the conversation.

## Agree/agree with

The word ***agree*** may look simple but it has several meanings when used in different situations. At one place its simple meaning is ***consent or yes.*** My proposal was really good so he ***agreed*** at once. When he asked me to help, I immediately ***agreed***. The meaning of ***agree with*** is ***be of the same opinion or be in harmony with.*** I hope you will ***agree with*** my new proposal. Yet there is another meaning of the term, ***agree with.*** It means ***match or confirm*** also. Your statement ***agrees with*** what has been said already. Your letter does not ***agree with*** what you had said earlier. In fact, at times we do use ***agree*** in different and varied situations without even knowing its implication. It is therefore, better to understand its varied uses and enrich your conversation.

## All of

The phrase ***all of*** has quite a different meaning than what ordinarily people know about it. It ***means everything or everyone.*** For example, "They wanted all or nothing." ***All of*** them wanted to join the party. But the simple meaning of ***all*** is ***whole number of. All*** cows are animals, but not ***all*** animals are cows. ***All*** also suggests at times ***what we value most***. For example, "I lost my ***all*** when I was a child." When two persons are conversing, at times they may use ***all*** without even understanding its meaning correctly. One of them may say it when agitated or emotionally charged, "I am prepared to give her/him all if she can agree to my proposal."

## Appeal to/for/against

It may simply mean ***make an earnest request***. The mother appealed to the principal of the school to pardon her son for his mistake. Social workers often appeal to the rich to help the poor. It is also used when someone makes ***an appeal (legal) against a decision***. The victim appealed against the judgement and requested to reopen his case. Another use of the term, ***appeal*** is made when it ***indicates movement of the feelings or indicates attraction or fascination.*** For example, The Prime Minister's speech appealed to the people. Bright colours often appeal to small children. Yet there is another meaning attached to the term, ***appeal. It indicates attraction or interest.*** Instrumental music has no appeal for me. Her arguments don't appeal to me. All the varied uses of ***appeal*** are related to different situations but are absolutely befitting during small conversations.

## Approve of

Its simple meaning is ***to give one's approval of.*** The CEO will never ***approve of*** your plan. I shall always ***approve of*** your marriage with Shyam. It also means ***to confirm or to agree to***. The President of the Society has ***approved*** the minutes ***of*** the meeting. That means the President being in agreement with the proceedings of the minutes, has confirmed the minutes. I don't like your plan, so I don't ***approve of*** it.

## Arrange/arrange for

It simply meant ***to put in order***. Please ***arrange*** the books on the shelves. They are arranging the furniture in the living room. ***Arrange for*** expresses the idea ***of making plans in advance***. She has ***arranged for*** a car to meet me at the railway station. ***Arrange for*** has another meaning, which is absolutely important to learn. It means ***to settle or to adjust***. The hostel warden often has to arrange for disputes between the inmates.

## As/as

The adverb ***as*** has several uses in spoken and written English. When another ***as*** is used in a sentence, it often ***indicates***

***a sort of comparison of the same degree***. I am ***as*** tall ***as*** you are. Is it ***as*** difficult to mount that hill ***as*** they say? Another meaning of ***as*** is to indicate ***when or while***. They saw her as she was getting off his car. It is also used to indicate ***since***. ***As*** he was tired, he did not accompany us. Thus, even very simple words like ***as*** has several uses in conversation. Besides, it has another very apt use while conversing with people. It means ***regard, view, represent or acknowledge***. Most people regarded him ***as*** a highly literate person.

## Attend to/ attend upon

***Attend to*** means ***to give care and thought.*** Please ***attend to*** your work carefully. It also means ***to listen carefully.*** The owner of the shop advises his workers to ***attend to*** the customers carefully. It means the workers should listen to their needs and supply material, as they desire. The meaning of to ***attend upon*** is ***to wait on, look after or to serve***. I have been ***attending upon*** my mother since she has been bedridden. When someone goes to see an ailing friend and he ***feels*** that the friend is ***improving***, he may say, "Well, it seems that the doctor is ***attending*** you well." It simply means that the doctor has been taking care of the friend and so he has been recovering.

## Avalanche

It means a ***great amount of snow and ice at a high altitude slide down from the top due*** to its own weight and cause lot of damage to the forests and houses. But during conversation, it is used figuratively. When someone in great anger ***speaks loudly and very fast and hurdles words without stopping***, one would say "An ***avalanche*** of words he hurdled upon me as he was so annoyed with what had happened." Some people are wont (used to) to speak without stopping and would go on saying words after words. You can say, "Oh, he expressed his feelings in words like an ***avalanche***."

## Babble out

It means ***to talk in a way difficult to comprehend***. It also means ***to make a sound like a baby.*** When someone is not able to speak clearly or when his/her words are not being understood well, one can say "You are babbling out so nothing is clear to me." It has another use too. It means ***a childish or foolish or confused talk***, which is not understood at all. Some people have the habit of ***babbling*** without knowing that they are not being comprehended at all.

## Back/back up/back down/ back out

Simple meaning of back is ***to go backward***. She backed her car out of the garage. ***Back up means support.*** I have a good friend who will ***back*** me ***up*** in my difficulties. Please ***back*** me ***up*** when we discuss that particular point in the meeting. The meaning of ***back down*** is ***to give up a claim.*** She has ***backed down*** from her position she took last week. While talking in a meeting someone said, "I don't want to continue as a Secretary of the Company any longer. So I ***back down*** from it today." ***Back out*** implies ***withdrawal from a promise or an undertaking.*** There are some people who first promise to help but later on they ***back out*** (withdraw). There are several uses of back when used as compounds. For example, when we say "He is my ***back bone"***, it means he is ***my only support.*** Thus, ***back*** though quite a simple expression, has several uncommon uses.

## Bar

The simple meaning of ***bar*** is a ***long piece of hard stiff material either made of wood or metal, etc.*** Strong bars are fitted to this door. The other meaning of bar is a ***barrier that could not be passed.*** It is a ***barrier that hinders or stops progress.*** Poverty may quite often be a ***bar*** to success. It could also mean a kind of ***railing dividing off the space.*** The ***bar*** placed in the middle of this room has divided it equally well. Bar ***means a profession of barristers*** too. It also means a place where drinks are served.

## Bear/ bear oneself/ bear against

It means that ***shows, reflects and contains.*** This document bears your signatures. This shirt ***bears*** the name of the company where it was made. He ***bears*** a good character. ***Bear oneself*** means ***carrying oneself in a specified way.*** He bears himself like a great actor. That means he ***stands,***

***walks and behaves like*** an actor. Bear against means ***having in the heart or mind.*** Please don't bear any grudge against your friends. During ordinary conversation, many people use such terms to denote someone's attitude towards others.

## Be

It simply ***indicates a change from one quality, place to another.*** She wants ***to be*** (become) a doctor. When it is used as a third form of the verb, it means ***already done or finished.*** I have ***been*** to Lucknow. It means I have visited or seen Lucknow. It is also used ***to denote progressive tense.*** What has she ***been*** doing this afternoon?

## Bend/bend towards/on

The simple meaning of ***bend*** is ***cause to be out of a straight line or to force into a curve.*** The cobbler bent the shoe to make it more useable. A friend asking another friend when he requires his help, "Please ***bend a little*** to the other side to make me more comfortable. The second meaning of ***bend*** is ***to become curved.*** The branches of the trees were ***bent with*** the weight of the fruits they had been bearing. Yet there is another meaning of ***bend*** when followed by towards. It means ***turn towards.*** It is very late now. Let us ***bend*** our steps towards home. It also provides ***the meaning of determination.*** He is ***bent on*** learning driving. She is ***bent on*** (upon) attaining very high marks in the examination.

## Beside/besides

The simple meaning of ***beside*** is ***by the side of or close to.*** I would like to stay ***beside*** you. He would like to live beside a hillock. Please sit beside me. It has another expression involved. It means ***compared with.*** You are quite healthy ***beside*** your other brother. There is yet another meaning contained in the term, ***beside***. It conveys ***end of one's control or highly emotional.*** I was ***beside*** myself when I heard the good news. But ***besides*** has also different meanings involved. It means ***moreover, also and as well.*** I don't like that sight for a new house; ***besides***, it is quite far away as well. We are three brothers ***besides*** Mohan. (Mohan is not included in the three) He had no time to attend the meeting. ***Besides***, he was unwell. Thus, the reader should know that by adding the letter 's' to ***beside***, the expression altogether changes.

## Better/ for better or/ to better

The term ***better*** has many expressions involved. It simply indicates a ***kind of comparison.*** For example, "This dress is good but the other one is ***better.***" Discretion is the ***better*** part of valour. It also means ***the more.*** The ***better*** I know him the more I understand him. When we use the term, ***better of*** it implies ***overcoming or winning***. His aggressiveness got the ***better of*** him. It means he became aggressive rather than he should have not been (aggressive) at a particular moment. The term ***to better*** implies ***to***

***improve or do better***. The doctor hopes ***to better*** the conditions of the patients.

## Bid for/ bid up/bid on

In fact, the word ***bid*** has so many connotations when suffixed with prepositions like for, up and on, etc. The simple meaning of ***bid for*** is to ***make an offer of money.*** Will you like to ***bid for*** this house? To ***bid up*** means to ***make the price higher*** by offering more money. The red mansion was ***bid up*** far beyond its real value. The meaning of the term ***bid on*** is ***to put in a tender for.*** The contractor decided to ***bid on*** the new building. The rich man chose to ***bid on*** the old car, as he liked it most.

## Blow/blow in/into/blow off/ blow over/blow out

The simple meaning of ***blow*** is ***to move along***. It was blowing hard. It means the ***wind was blowing hard***. The wind blew the chairs off to the shore. ***Blow in*** is used to convey the ***arrival of someone/something quite noisily or suddenly.*** Satish opened the door and ***blew in/into*** the room. ***Blow off*** is used ***to convey releasing the tension.*** Teachers must let their students ***blow off*** steam sometimes. It means teachers need to permit students to talk freely at times so that they may be able to convey their grievances of which teachers are not aware of. ***Blow over*** means ***to be forgotten***. The hard days will soon ***blow over. Blow out*** means to ***exhaust itself.*** The wind has ***blown*** itself ***out.*** His anger was finally ***blown out.***

## Board/above board/across the board/ boarding

In fact, the term ***board*** carries several meanings when prefixed or suffixed with some prepositions. The simple meaning of ***board*** is ***a flat piece of wood with square edges***. It can be used in making buildings, etc. When we use the term ***above board***, it indicates ***openly without any deception.*** The Chief Minister of the Sate is ***above board***. It means he is not deceptive and secretive. ***Across the board*** implies ***food served at table, especially meals supplied by the week or month as a part of the payment for service. Boarding*** means ***living***. She is ***boarding*** with her cousin.

## Bore

When it is used as a verb, it means ***to make a narrow, round and deep hole with a tool.*** They are making a bore to find out how deep they need to go to find water in the ground. ***Bore*** also implies ***feeling tired by being dull***. Are you getting bored here? Most of these tales have ***bored*** me for they don't have much exciting material in them. Yet ***bore*** also indicates ***high tidal waves often many feet high.*** Oh, look at those ***bore*** invading the shore.

## Bound/bound to/ bound for

Simple meaning of ***bound*** is ***limit.*** It is beyond my ***bounds to*** complete that task. She is very ambitious. There are no ***bounds to*** it. It means her ambitions are extremely high. The other meaning of ***bound*** is ***to jump, spring or bounce, move or run in jumping movements.*** Her heart ***bounded*** with joy. ***Bound for*** is used to convey ***ready to start/go.*** The train is bound for Lucknow, which simply means that its destination is Lucknow.

## Brake

This simple word has several meanings and can be used in different situations. Its simple meaning is ***a devise for reducing speed or even stopping motion or control something.*** Please apply ***break*** to your anger. Apply ***brakes*** to reduce the speed of your car. It also means ***a large wagon or open carriage.*** They are enjoying a pleasure trip in a ***brake***.

## Break/break into/break off/break out/ break through/break away

When someone gets bored or disturbed by some problem created by a friend or wife or husband, one of them can use such a term ***to get some space of time to relax***. Give me ***a break.*** I am so tired with everything. The term ***break*** conveys the same meaning as 'brake' used in old English. You need to apply some ***break*** to your tongue. ***Break into*** means ***to force one's way into.*** Some thieves broke into my neighbour's house last night. ***Break off*** implies ***to stop speaking***. It also means ***to stop temporarily***. Let us ***break off*** the meeting for one hour to plan the budget once again. ***Break out*** implies ***sudden appearance or start***. Riots ***broke out*** between the two communities last night. The fire ***broke out*** in the evening around seven. ***Break through*** implies ***to make a way through.*** The police broke through the locked house when no movement was perceptible in it for hours. ***Break away*** means ***to go away suddenly, or abruptly.*** "Can you ***break away*** from smoking so suddenly"? The captives ***broke away*** from the guards.

## Bring/bring about/bring back/ bring out/bring round

Its simple meaning is ***to carry or to take or cause to produce. Bring*** me a glass of water. Please bring Sheela to the party with you. ***Bring about*** means ***cause to happen.*** The Prime Minister ***brought about*** many changes in the Constitution. ***Bring back*** conveys ***to return or cause to remember***. Please don't forget to bring me back my book. Your last letter ***brought*** me ***back*** (reminded me) many old memories. ***Bring out*** sustains a sense ***to appear or to show clearly***. The publisher will ***bring out*** the new edition of the book soon. ***Bring round*** means ***to cause or regain consciousness or to yield.*** She was not keen to disclose her intentions but we managed to ***bring*** her ***round***.

## But/but for

***But*** has several uses in English language. It can be used in different situations. It implies ***only*** as well as it is used ***to coordinating*** as a conjunction. All were present in the function ***but*** (except/only) you. She tried to perform her best ***but*** she could not. You all are wrong in this situation ***but*** me. ***But for*** implies ***except for, without***. We would have ruined ***but*** for your help.

## Care/care about/care for/care to

The simple meaning of ***care*** is ***to pay serious attention or thought.*** For example, "Please take *care* of this article. It is fragile." "You must take ***care*** when you go across the street as these days there is a lot of traffic". ***Care about*** implies ***to feel interest, anxiety or sorrow.*** She failed in the examination but she does not *care about* it. ***Care for*** is used to show one's ***liking or to have something***. Would you please ***care for*** a cup of tea? ***Care to*** imply ***willingness or liking***. I don't ***care to*** go for a walk at this hour.

## Carry/ carry with/carry far/carry away/carry back/carry forward

Its simple meaning is ***to support the weight of and move from one place to another.*** He carried the chair across the floor. She was ***carrying*** a file with her. It also means ***to wear or to have with one.*** He always ***carries*** an umbrella with him. It also means ***support***. These pillars ***carry*** the weight of the bridge. ***Carry far*** means ***make longer or***

***extend.*** He cannot carry far with his responsibilities. ***Carry away*** means to ***causing to lose.*** The boat was carried away by the waves. ***Carry back*** means ***to take or keep back in the memory, to recall.*** Your story carried me back to my school days. ***Carry forward*** means ***to transfer to the head of a new page.*** Please carry these figures forward.

## Case/in case/ in case of/in any case

The word ***case*** signifies a box, bag, covering or a container. It also means the ***actual state of affairs or instance.*** It is a clear ***case of*** cheating. Is that the case that she has lost all her property? ***In case*** means 'if it should happen that.' In case he forgets his promise, just remind him. ***In case of*** implies ***in the event of.*** In case of floods, please inform the police at once. ***In any case*** is used to convey ***whatever happens or may have happened.*** For example, "In any case whether she gets through the examinations or she does not, you must inform me."

## Catch/catch up/catch on

It simply means ***stopping by getting hold of something*** by hands. The wicketkeeper ***caught*** the player by diving towards the ***catch.*** She is always on time to ***catch*** a train. It also indicates ***an act of catching.*** Today you had a good catch of fish while fishing. ***Catch up*** means ***overtaking.*** Even if you start earlier by your car, I can always ***catch*** you ***up.*** If you are left behind in studies in your class, work hard to ***catch up*** your other friends. ***Catch on*** implies ***to get the***

***meaning of or to understand.*** At times, I don't quite ***catch*** you ***on*** as you speak too softly. It means you speak very slowly so the listener does not *get* (understand) you.

## Certain/ certain of/ certainly/for certain

The simple meaning of ***certain*** is ***settled; of which there is no doubt.*** It is ***certain*** that he will reach home tonight. It also implies the ***sense of confidence*** too. I am ***certain of*** that he saw me when I was coming out of the shop. It also implies ***to possess a definite knowledge about something. For certain*** conveys the meaning ***to be without any doubt.*** I know ***for certain*** when she will come home. ***Certainly*** also implies the ***sense of definiteness***. If you need my help, certainly, I shall come forward for it. Thus, more or less, the term ***certain*** conveys a definite attitude of mind; it conveys a kind of conviction or determination in the mind of the person who uses it.

## Change/change to/change for/change over/change from

It means ***leave one place and go to enter another; take off or put on***. Please change these shoes, as they look dirty. ***Change*** your clothes at once. When you feel that the car has slowed down and not pulling its weight, ***change to*** a higher gear. I don't like to ***change for*** dinner. It means I don't like to wear a formal dress to go for dinner. ***Change over*** is used ***to convey abandoning old system to a new one***. I have ***changed over*** from the old traditional way of thinking to a new and modern way. ***Change from*** conveys ***make or become different.*** The traffic lights have ***changed*** from red to green only two seconds before. Thus, the reader will find that the term/word ***change*** has several uses in the language. It conveys ***changed*** or ***different conditions and is used in place of another or others.*** She purchased a big house. It's a great ***change for*** the better.

## Charge/in charge

It conveys ***to state that a person has done wrong or broken the law.*** He has been ***charged*** last week for driving through the red light. It also conveys ***a sudden or violent attack at a high speed.*** The Indian forces ***charged*** the enemy lines at midnight on Tuesday. A black dog ***charged*** me in the street last night. The term ***in charge*** conveys *about* ***work given or a position of responsibility,*** etc. These days, Mr. Paliwal is ***in*** (under) ***charge*** of the college. It also implies the meaning ***to become responsible for***. Sheela was put ***in*** the doctor's ***charge.***

## Check/check in/check out/check upon

The simple word ***check*** has various uses in the language. It simply means ***examining something to learn whether it is correct.*** Please ***check*** the totals whether they are correct. ***Check*** also means ***to hold back or to stop.*** You must ***check*** your emotions. ***Check in*** means ***to register in a hotel at one's arrival.*** Did you ***check in*** the hotel and put your address correctly? ***Check out*** is commonly used ***when one***

***leaves a hotel after clearing the accounts. Check upon*** conveys the meaning ***to have control.*** When the wind blows hard, it often ***checks upon*** the rain.

## Clean/clean out/clean up

It simply means ***free from dirt.*** Put some ***clean*** sheets on the bed after removing the dirty ones. It also implies ***purity, innocence and free from wrongdoing.*** Sri Ram Krishan led a ***clean*** life. It also means ***skilful, smart.*** The wicketkeeper took ***a clean*** catch. Clean out conveys ***winning or taking all the money.*** She ***cleaned*** me ***out*** by her tricks. ***Clean up*** means ***to put in order.*** The Superintendent of Police ***cleaned up*** the town from the thieves. They ***cleaned up*** the room after midnight when the party was over.

## Clear/clear about/clear of/ clear from/clear out

It simply means ***free from obstruction; easily seen.*** It is a ***clear*** photograph. ***Clear*** means ***free from guilt or blame.*** He seems to possess a ***clear*** conscience. ***Clear*** means ***distinctly.*** Why can't you talk clearly? ***Clear about*** conveys the meaning of ***free from doubt or difficulty. It also involves certainty.*** She delivered a ***clear*** speech. My thoughts are not ***clear about*** the issue. ***Clear of*** means ***free from suspicion or doubt.*** The officer said, "You are now ***clear of*** suspicion." ***Clear from*** means ***to remove, get rid of what is not needed.*** Please ***clear*** your mind ***from*** any doubts.

***Clear out*** conveys the sense of ***going away or leaving.*** She is after you. Better you ***clear out***. It means better you leave before she gets you. Thus, ***clear*** involves so many meanings in different situations.

## Close/close up/close by/close down

It means ***near in space or time***. You are standing quite ***close*** to me. ***Close*** has another meaning too. It simply means ***to shut.*** Please ***close*** the doors tightly. Close also indicates ***end or conclusion of a period or time.*** It is the time ***to close*** the play. ***Close up*** is used ***to show a close view***. Please take a ***close up*** of the scene to know the details. In fact, ***close*** is used with many suffixes, such as, ***close order*** (marching with not much space), in ***close confidence***, ***close consideration, close attention***, ***close context***, etc. As a prefix, the word ***close*** implies the meaning ***great*** or ***much***. Thus, ***close confidence*** would mean ***great confidence*** and ***close attention*** means ***much attention***. ***Close by*** means ***near***. She lives ***close by*** my house. ***Close down*** is used ***to indicate shutting down a business or a factory or a shop***. The shop was ***closed down*** because of lack of business. The bus-stand ***closes down*** after midnight.

## Control/control of/control (on) over

It means ***power or authority to direct, order or check.*** The principal of a school must keep the students and staff in ***control.*** Children, who don't have parents' ***control,*** are likely to be indisciplined. Children should be kept under the

***control of*** parents. ***Control over*** implies ***authority-management.*** The Prime Minister should have full ***control over*** his Cabinet. ***Control on*** also implies similar sort of ***authority or restraint***. She has no ***control on*** (***over***) her children.

## Cool/cool down (off)

The simple meaning of ***cool*** is ***neither warm nor cold, but in between.*** Please sit under the shade of the tree and keep ***cool***. It also means ***calm or unexcited.*** Please throw away your anger and keep ***cool.*** It also reflects ***lack of interest or enthusiasm.*** We were received very ***coolly. Cool down*** (***off***) gives the sense of ***becoming or making cool.*** His anger ***cooled down*** after he received back his money. She has ***cooled down*** towards me. It means that she is no more interested in me.

## Cost/cost of/at all cost

It ***indicates price.*** It is not used in passive voice. The car ***cost*** me Rupees 3 Lakh. Its one more use is quite important. ***Cost of*** implies considering ***risks and expenses***. They won the case but at the ***cost of*** losing everything. ***At all cost*** implies ***at the loss or expenses***. We must win this battle ***at all cost***.

## Course/course of/ in due course/of course

Course conveys the sense of ***chase*** or ***to move quickly***. As she was deeply hurt, tears ***coursed*** down her cheeks. The dogs ***coursed*** the cat very hard. It also identifies with ***forward movement in time and space***. In the ***course of*** my life, I have never tried to ditch anyone. This house is in the ***course of*** construction. ***In due course*** conveys the sense of ***natural order***. Although she had a bad accident, she will recover ***in due course*** of time. At times, the term, ***of course*** is used ***to confirm one's views or opinion*** in response to someone's query or inquiry. Will you please come along with me to the cinema tonight? In response, one can say, ***of course,*** which conveys one's strong agreement. Thus, the word ***course*** with some prefixes and suffixes provides various sorts of meanings that can make a conversation very interesting.

## Cry/cry off/cry out

It means persons, animals or birds making ***sounds expressing feelings of pain and fear.*** When I take her to hospital, she ***cries*** everytime. ***Cry off*** means ***withdrawing from that one has undertaken***. He had promised to help me, but had to ***cry off*** at the last moment. ***Cry out*** means ***crying until one gets emotional relief.*** Let him ***cry out*** until he feels relieved.

## Dare/dare to

Dare is used mainly in negative sentences, including those with *hardly, never* and *no one*. It, in fact, unfolds some sort of ***doubt***. For example, "Don't you ***dare to*** talk to me again." "No one ***dared*** to speak to him again." "How dare she enter my house without my permission?" ***Dare*** also implies the meaning of being ***brave enough***. He has never ***dared to*** tell me all that. It also ***suggests courage***. I ***dare*** you ***to*** say it again.

## Deny

This word is used to indicate that ***it is not true***. Someone who is being accused can say, 'I ***deny*** the charges.' It also means ***to refuse to acknowledge or disown.*** He ***denied*** that he went to her place last night. She ***denied*** that it was her signatures. Yet ***deny*** has one more meaning. It implies ***to refuse to give.*** She does not ***deny*** anything to her children. That means whatever the children ask, she yields to their request. I was ***denied*** admittance in the hall as it was full by the time I reached there. People often use deny to say 'no' in place of ***refuse***. The reader must keep in mind the difference in the meanings of the two words, 'deny' and 'refuse.' Refusal involves unwillingness, (which means to say 'no'), but 'deny' has all the above referred to meanings.

## Desert

It simply means ***to leave or go away***. The streets were ***deserted*** by midnight, as people feared that there could be riots. It also means ***to leave without support or help***. She ***deserted*** her husband and went away. Soldiers are not supposed ***to desert*** their Units anytime. If they do so, they will be punished. ***Desert*** has another meaning, which implies ***to fail.*** My courage ***deserted*** me when I saw a ghostly figure in the dark. There is one more meaning involved with the term, ***desert***. It means ***a large area of barren land.*** It is one of the precious words in the language that can be used intelligently to enrich conversation.

## Design/design for

Design means ***drawing or outline from which something can be made or drawn.*** It also means ***a general arrangement or planning*** of a picture, building, machine, etc. This machine has a faulty ***design,*** therefore, it is not working as desired. It also means ***a pattern, arrangement of lines, shapes, details,*** etc. The face of this building has some beautiful ***designs*** containing flowers and sketches of human figures. I saw Leela wearing a beautiful dress with an attractive ***design*** on it. ***Design for*** means ***intend to*** or ***planned to.*** This college is ***designed for*** creating/making excellent architects. It also means ***purpose***. She ***designed*** this extra room in the house to house her guests.

## Die/die from/die for/die hard/die away

It is a block of ***hard metal with a design***, cut in it to use for shaping coins, medals, etc. It also means ***to come to the end of life or cease to live.*** Two soldiers ***died from*** their wounds last evening. A real patriot will never hesitate to ***die for*** his/her country. ***Die hard*** means ***to die only after struggle.*** It is used when a person ***obstinately resists being compelled to do anything***. He ***died hard*** to reveal any secrets against his country. ***Die away*** means ***to lose strength or to become weak.*** The wind gradually ***died away***. After the midnight, the noise ***died away***.

## Direct/direct to (towards)

Its simple meaning is ***straight, not curbed.*** They are going in a ***straight*** line. It also implies the meaning of ***straightforwardness or going straight to the point.*** The Prime Minister gave a ***direct*** answer to all the questions posed by the media. Direct also implies, ***how to do, or how to get somewhere.*** Please ***direct*** me to the railway station. ***Direct to*** means ***to speak to or to put address or remarks.*** He ***directed*** the document ***to*** his home address. It also possesses the meaning of ***to manage or to control.*** Raj Kapoor ***directed*** the film, *Sangam*. Without much thinking, our steps were ***directed towards*** home. The boss ***directed*** his men to proceed ***towards*** the building.

## Divide up/out/divide into/by

It means ***to separate or break up.*** Please ***divide up*** the work before starting it. Can you ***divide*** fifty ***into*** five parts? Fifty can be ***divided by*** ten into five parts. It also conveys the sense ***to (cause) parting for some purpose***. My friends don't seem to be ***divided*** on this issue. The simple meaning of ***divide*** is just ***to divide*** or ***that divides.*** This straight line in the middle of the room ***divides*** it into two.

## Down/down to/up and down/ get down/ups and downs

It means ***from a higher level to a lower level.*** The flag was taken ***down*** at the end of the ceremony. The sun went ***down*** in the evening around six. She was knocked ***down*** by a scooter. It also means ***to indicate a state of less activity.*** The temperature has gone ***down***. The wind died ***down***. It also indicates ***period from an earlier time to a later time.*** Please read the history of India from fifteen hundred ***down to*** two thousand AD. It also means ***to and fro***. She is walking ***up and down*** for the last fifteen minutes. ***Get down to*** work means ***to start work in real earnest.*** You have wasted a lot of time so far. Better ***get down to*** work right now. ***Ups and downs*** indicate ***changes in one's fortune.*** Mohan had a number of ***ups and downs*** in his whole life. It means several times he was rich and poor as well.

## Drop/drop into, drop down/drop at/drop off/drop out/drop in on (drop by)

It means ***fall or cause to fall.*** There was total silence in the room. You could easily hear a pin ***drop***. The room temperature ***dropped*** down suddenly after the cooler started working. ***Dropped into*** or ***dropped down*** is used ***to indicate fall*** or ***sink to the ground.*** He was too tired so he ***dropped into*** the chair. She was almost ready to ***drop down*** with fatigue. It also means ***to stop, to allow, to get out***. Please

***drop*** me ***at*** the hospital. ***Drop off*** indicates ***to become fewer or less.*** Her visits have ***dropped off*** these days. The doctor's practice has ***dropped off*** recently. Now he has fewer patients visiting him. ***Drop out*** means ***cease to compete, not to take part, give up the idea***. I am ***dropping out*** from the race as I feel I am not fit to run. ***Drop in on*** means ***to pay a short visit.*** Please ***drop in on*** whenever you like. She ***dropped by*** to see me yesterday.

## Drive/drive hard/drive at

Drive means ***driving or being driven (not in a public vehicle).*** The airport is an hour's ***drive*** from here. The connotation ***driving hard*** conveys the meaning, ***to put pressure on someone***. For example, if one of my friends or relatives presses me hard to do some work/job and if I don't have time or don't like to do it right at that time, and pressure is being put on, I can say, ***you are driving me hard.*** Give me a break. But the simple meaning of ***driving hard*** would be to ***drive fast***. ***Drive*** also means ***energy, capacity to get things done.*** The principal is lacking in ***drive***. ***Drive at*** mean, ***intent***. What is she ***driving at*** is not clear to me.

## Ease/at ease/ ill at ease/with ease/ ease of

The simple meaning of ***ease*** is ***freedom from work, discomfort, trouble, difficulty or anxiety.*** She lives a life of ***ease***. She has an ***easy*** life. Please stand ***at ease***. It means ***stand relaxed***. ***Ill at ease*** conveys the sense of ***to be anxious***

***or embarrassed***. He seemed to be ***ill at ease*** after the lecture. ***With ease*** conveys the meaning of ***without any difficulty***. He helped me ***with ease***. ***Ease of*** conveys the sense of ***give relief to***. Can I ***ease*** you ***of*** with your problems?

## Enter/enter into/enter on (upon)/enter for

It means ***come or go into***. The carriage entered the building. ***Enter into*** means ***to begin***; ***to open***. When I ***entered into*** conversation, the atmosphere was already hot. ***Enter on*** means ***make a start on (upon) a new career***. Sheela ***entered upon*** a new career on last Tuesday when she joined the Bar. She has ***entered for*** Master's examination this year.

## Excess/in excess of/to excess

It means ***fact of being amount by which it is more than expected, not proper***. The conductor of the bus said to the passenger, "Sir, your luggage is ***in excess of*** ten kilograms. It should have been 20 kilograms, where as you have almost thirty kilograms." ***To excess*** conveys the sense of ***to an extreme degree***. When his mother died, he carried his grief ***to excess***.

## Excuse/ excuse for/in excuse of/excuse from

It means ***reason given to explain or defend one's conduct***. Please ***excuse*** me for her conduct. She is always late for her lectures but every time she makes a good ***excuse for*** her lateness. Where the rule is concerned, she cannot plead ignorant ***in excuse of*** her conduct. ***Excuse from*** means ***free***

***from a duty or requirement.*** He was ***excused from*** attending the last lecture as he had some other duty to perform.

## Face/face to face/in the face/ save face/ on the face of it

The simple meaning of face is the front part of head, eyes, cheeks, mouth, etc. It also means ***to have or turn the face to***. Please turn round and ***face*** them. ***Face to face*** implies ***to bring two persons (parties) to confront one another***. It is better to bring them ***face to face*** so that the truth maybe revealed. ***Save face*** means ***refrain from or to evade to shame oneself openly.*** The President of the Club did not attend the meeting to ***save his face***, as there were many people who were ready to put charges of corruption against him. ***On the face of it*** implies ***judging by appearance. On the face of it,*** her arguments don't seem to be convincing. You can judge a person's intent ***on the face of it*** by his arguments.

## Fall/ fall down (over)/ fall short/ fall flat/ fall on (upon/to)/fall in (into)/ fall out

Fall means ***act of falling.*** She ***fell*** from her horse. ***Fall down*** (over) means ***come or go down freely***. She ***fell over*** into the pond. ***Fall short*** means ***not going far enough***. Her efforts ***fell short*** of our expectations. ***Fall flat*** means ***fail to have intended effect.*** His most articles ***fell flat,*** as they did not have the intended effect. They made such an awful programme that it ***fell flat***. Nobody liked it. ***Fall upon*** means ***descend upon.*** After a while, all were quiet. A great silence ***fell upon*** the audience. ***Fall on*** conveys the meaning ***coming by chance, design or right***. All the expenses of his daughter's marriage ***fell on*** the relatives, who had come to attend the marriage. ***Fall out*** conveys the sense of ***going off parade, happen.*** It so ***fell out*** that she could not attend the programme, as scheduled. ***Fall in (into) means to be included*** within the ***range or scope of something***. The specimens ***fall into*** three categories. ***Fell in*** also conveys to begin or start. She ***fell in*** love with a poor boy.

## Far/far from/go far/far and away/ far off

***Far*** indicates ***a great distance***. How ***far*** did she travel? ***Far from*** is used ***to indicate instead of.*** The quality of your work is ***far from*** satisfactory. It means it is of very poor quality. ***Go far*** means be ***successful, do much.*** Mohan is intelligent and hard working. He will surely ***go far.*** It means he is going to get great success in life. ***Far and away*** means ***by a large amount or degree***. Amitabh Bachchan is ***far and away*** the best actor so far seen on the Indian screen. ***Far off*** means ***far away.*** By midnight, he must have gone ***far away.***

## Fear/for fear of

It means a ***feeling of fear caused by the possibility of danger.*** When she saw the beast, she started trembling with ***fear***. ***For fear of*** means ***feeling of fear involved because of anxiety or tension.*** The doctor asked the visitors to keep quiet ***for fear of*** waking the patient who was in serious condition.

## Finish/finish up/finish off

***Finish*** means ***bring or come to an end***. She has not ***finished*** her work yet. ***Finish up*** means ***eat up completely***. She has finished up her dinner. ***Finish off*** may mean ***kill or destroy.*** That long illness nearly ***finished*** me ***off.***

## Gear/gear up-gear down

Toothed wheel as a part of a machine to connect the engine. We call such a part of the machine as a ***gear.*** It helps the driver to put the engine in different positions and makes it running at different speed. Please put the car in the first ***gear,*** as there is a great elevation ahead. ***Gear up and down*** mean change up and down or ***adjust one thing to the working of another***. You must ***gear up*** your economic status to be *at par* with the other people of status. Please learn to put right ***gears*** before you start learning driving.

## Get/get done/get about/get along/get away/ get down to/get it down

***Get*** means (to cause oneself to) ***become; pass from one state to another***. It is very cold here these days, but soon you will ***get*** used to it. ***Get done*** means ***to complete it***. Jack ***got*** his painting ***done*** before the end of last month.

***Get about*** means to ***be no longer confined.*** Though the news of his engagement was kept secret, soon it ***got about***. ***Get along*** means ***manage***. How do you ***get along*** with your new boss? ***Get away*** means ***manage to leave.*** The thieves ***got away*** with jewellery and lot of cash from the neighbour's house yesterday. ***Get down to*** means leave the table after the meals. As soon as they finished up the meals, they all ***got down***. ***Get it down*** also refers to swallow. The drink was so bitter that she could not ***get it down.*** Get down also *means* ***to begin*** or ***start***. For example, 'After a short nap, they ***got down*** to their jobs again.'

## Go from (to)/ go a long way/go very far/ go too far/ go along with/go down

The simple verb ***go*** provides different meanings when used in different situations. If you say, "With your bad habits, you cannot ***go*** very far." Here its meaning is ***not making much progress***. It also means ***to leave***. Just ***go*** now. It means just leave the place. ***Go a long way*** means make ***a considerable contribution towards something***. His father's advice ***went a long way*** to help him improve his life. ***Go very far*** means ***last.*** The rupee does not ***go very far*** these days. It simply means it does not buy much. ***Go too far*** means to ***go beyond acceptable limits***. ***Go along with*** means ***accompany*** or ***agree with***. She did not ***go along with*** me too far after dinner. I cannot ***go along with*** you as far as this plan is concerned. ***Go down*** simply means ***sink*** or ***be swallowed***. The wind has ***gone down*** after the midday. This drink is so bitter that it wouldn't ***go down*** my throat.

## Hold/ hold breath/ hold it down/ hold off/ hold on/hold out/hold it over/hold up

It means ***to have or keep in one's possession.*** His mother was ***holding*** a purse in her hand. ***Hold breath*** is used to convey ***holding breath from excitement or fear***. ***Hold down*** conveys the meaning ***to keep it down or under***. The Finance Minister has been trying hard to ***hold the prices down. Hold off*** means ***to remain at a distance***. I hope the rain will ***hold off*** until we finish our dinner. ***Hold on*** means ***to stand firm when there is danger.*** If a tide comes down, you cannot ***hold on*** here for long. ***Hold out*** has two different meanings— ***above*** or ***offer***. She has been constantly working hard. It ***holds out*** some hope of success. ***Hold it over*** means ***to defer, to postpone***. The meeting was ***held over*** until Monday next. ***Hold up*** provides the meaning of ***delay***. The passengers were ***held up*** for two hours at the bus stand on account of heavy rains.

## Inquire/inquire about/inquire after/inquire into

It means ***asked to be told***. Sir, I want to ***inquire about*** a particular person. ***Inquire about*** means ***ask for information about.*** Please go to the railway station and ***inquire about*** the trains that go to Delhi from Agra. ***Inquire after*** means ***ask about.*** I want to ***inquire after*** her health. ***Inquire***

***into*** means ***try to learn the facts about; investigate.*** You should ***inquire into*** the matter immediately.

## Join/join hands/ join up/join in

It means ***put together; unite; connect.*** Please ***join*** these two tables together. ***Join hands*** (clasping hands) means ***combine in an enterprise.*** If you ***join hands*** with me in my company, we can progress with a great speed. ***Join in*** means ***to come into the company*** or ***be a part of it***. Can I ***join in*** the game in the middle of it?

## Keep/ keep back/ keep away/keep down/ keep off/ keep up/keep out

Keep means cause to remain. Keep it with you. ***Keep back*** means not letting others to know about it. ***Keep*** the news ***back*** unto you. Don't let others know about it. ***Keep away*** means ***prevent from going***. ***Keep away*** from fire. ***Keep down*** means ***hold in subjection.*** The prisoners were ***kept down*** in the prison. ***Keep off*** means ***remain at a distance***. I advise you to ***keep off*** the rioting people. ***Keep up*** means ***to go forward at the same pace, speed up***. Please don't lag behind. Walk at a speed so as to ***keep up*** with others. ***Keep out*** means ***remain outside***. Please don't get involved in that affair. ***Keep out*** of it.

## Kick/kick back/kick off/ kick against/kick out

It means the ***act of kicking***. Please give a ***kick*** at the bathroom door for one who is in has taken so much time to come out of it. ***Kick back*** means ***percentage of payment made*** to one who has been instrumental to make money. It *is* ***a kind of bribe money***. ***Kick off*** means ***to start the game*** or to remove by kicking off. The captain ***kicked off*** the ball to start the game. ***Kick against*** means ***to show annoyance***. She ***kicked against*** his advice for she thought he was wrong. ***Kick out*** means ***to expel*** or get out. As he was drunk, the hotel manager ***kicked*** him ***out*** of his room.

## Knock/knock down/knock out/knock about/ knock on/ knock up

***Knock*** means ***blow***. Last night as the lights were off, she got a hard ***knock*** on her forehead when she was walking across the room. ***Knock down*** means ***strike to the ground*** or ***floor***. When he was trying to cross the road, a car ***knocked*** him ***down***. ***Knock out*** is used to indicate the ***defeat of a player*** by another one. The Russian boxer ***knocked out*** the Afghan boxer in the last round. ***Knock about*** means leading an unsettled life, travelling and living in various places. Satish has ***knocked about*** all over the country. ***Knock on*** means to ***move or kick forward***. ***Knock*** the ball ***on*** towards the goal before it goes out. ***Knock up*** means ***waken or rouse***. Please ***knock*** me ***up*** at seven in the morning so that I can catch the train.

## Lay/lay hands on/lay hopes/lay to rest/lay bare/lay aside/lay down/lay off/lay over

***Lay*** may mean ***to put on a surface*** or ***to put in a proper position***. ***Lay hands*** on means to ***get possession of***. She is very greedy. She takes everything away, she can ***lay hands on***. ***Lay hopes*** indicate ***to pin one's hopes on***. Hari's mother ***lays*** all her ***hopes on*** him, as he is the only earning member in the family. ***Lay to rest*** means to ***bury***. Margaret was ***laid to rest*** in the church last evening. ***Lay bare*** means to ***show or reveal.*** Soon she started crying and ***laid*** herself ***bare*** before him. ***Lay aside*** means to keep for future. Better you should ***lay*** some money ***aside*** for children. ***Lay down*** means ***to establish.*** The merchants have ***laid down*** the prices of the commodities. ***Lay off*** means ***to discontinue work or activity***. It also means ***to dismiss temporarily***. The master told the boy ***to lay off*** for a month. The workers were ***laid off*** on account of excessive heat. ***Lay over*** means ***to stop at a place during a journey***. You can make a ***lay over*** at the next town if you are very tired.

## Leave/leave for/leave alone/leave over/leave it behind

***Leave*** means ***to go away from***. I am ***leaving*** this town tomorrow morning. ***Leave for*** means ***to go away to***. She will be ***leaving for*** Mumbai in an hour from now. ***Leave alone*** conveys the meaning of ***not interfering with***. ***Leave*** me ***alone*** right now. ***Leave*** that child ***alone***. It would mean ***don't tease*** or ***disturb the child***. ***Leave over*** also means to ***postpone something***. Better ***leave*** your decision ***over*** for sometime. ***Leave it behind*** means ***to forget or neglect to bring*** or ***to take***. I ***left*** *my books* ***behind.*** Please don't ***leave*** her ***behind***.

## Let/let it be/live and let live/let it go

***Let*** means ***allow to.*** Please ***let*** me know what she told you about me. ***Let it be*** means to ***allow*** or ***to be quiet*** or ***unworried***. ***Let the poor man be*** there. Don't bother him. ***Live and let live*** involves ***the sense of permission*** or and ***assumption***. ***Let*** them all come. ***Let*** her do her best in the examination. ***Let it go*** means ***to release one's hold on***. Please ***let the ball go*** to your opponent. ***Let the rope go*** (release it).

## Lock/Lock it in/ lock it out/lock it up

***Lock*** means ***fasten a door or a box with a lock***. ***Lock it in*** means ***put in a box and lock it***. Please ***lock*** your jewellery ***in*** before you leave the house. ***Lock it out*** means ***keeping it outside*** or ***preventing it from entering***. It also means preventing the workmen to enter their place of work. If she does not come back before midnight, she will be ***locked out***. ***Lock it up*** means ***keeping it in the lock to make it safe.*** Better ***lock up*** your valuables properly.

## Look at/to look at/look back at/look good/look well/look about/look after/look down/look forward to/look in/look over/look through

***Look at*** means ***to use one's sight; turn the eyes in some direction*** or ***try to see***. Please ***look at*** the picture hanging on the wall. Similarly, ***look down*** and look up provide the meaning of ***looking downward*** or ***upward. To look at*** *him* would give the meaning of ***judging one from the outward appearance***. ***Look back at*** gives the sense of ***looking at angrily.*** He ***looked back at*** her instantly. ***Look good*** simply conveys sense of ***being attractive***. You ***look good*** in this dress. ***Look well*** gives the meaning of ***being healthy in appearance***. Today, she was ***looking well.*** It means she looked healthy that day. ***Look about*** means ***be on the watch; in search of.*** Is she still ***looking about*** for a job in the newspapers? ***Look after*** involves the sense of ***taking care of*** or ***watch over***. Who will ***look after*** the children when you leave for Pune ? ***Look down*** means ***despise*** or ***consider oneself superior***. It is seen that the rich mostly ***look down*** upon the poor. ***Look forward*** means to anticipate. He is ***looking forward*** to meet you again. ***Look in*** means ***making a short visit***. Please ***look in*** when you visit our town next. ***Look over means to inspect.*** Better we should ***look over*** the papers once again before coming to any conclusion. ***Look through*** involves the meaning ***to revise or to examine***. You must ***look through*** these bills before you decide to pay. Thus, the word ***look*** provides great meanings during conversation or in writing by suffixing some preposition or adjectives.

## Lose/lose ground/lose heart/lose sight of/ lose track

***Lose*** simply means ***no longer in possession*** or ***have taken away from one by accident***. She ***lost*** her job last week only. It means she was dismissed last week. Lose ground means ***no longer in the position of winning***. The lawyer argued erroneously that made him ***lose ground*** and eventually, he lost the case. ***Lose heart*** means ***to get disappointed or to lose courage***. She ***lost heart*** when she knew that she did not fare well in the examination. ***Lose sight*** means ***fail to take account***. We ***lost sight*** of the right track in the darkness and reached our destination after three hours. ***Lose track*** conveys the meaning ***to fail to hear***. The Finance Minister spoke so speedily that I often ***lost track*** with him and started getting bored.

## Make/make it from/make out/make believe/make sense/make shift/make after/ make away with/make out

***Make*** means ***construct or produce***. She ***made*** a cup of tea for me. ***Make,*** in fact gives several meanings in different situations. It means ***to establish*** or ***to enact too***. The school ***made*** rules to protect children. It also means ***to have*** or ***to eat***. She ***made*** a good lunch before they left. It also means

***to be intended.*** Harish and Roma live so happily as if they are ***made for*** each other. It also gives the sense of ***to become or cause to be.*** She ***made*** her intentions clear. ***Make it from*** means producing by combining materials. Wine is ***made from*** grapes. ***Make out*** means ***to deduce.*** Can you ***make out*** anything from this letter? ***Make believe*** means ***to pretend*** or ***pretence.*** Let us ***make believe*** that we are unable to do anything right now. ***Make sense*** means ***to provide meaning.*** This document does not ***make*** any ***sense*** when all was decided beforehand orally. ***Make shift*** is ***used for a time until better things are available.*** Please use this box as ***a make shift*** for a chair. ***Make after*** means ***to pursue*** or ***to chase.*** He ***made after*** the thief like a policeman. ***Make away with*** means ***to commit suicide.*** He ***made away with*** himself out of desperation. ***Make out*** means ***to complete*** or ***to fill in.*** Please ***make out*** a list of the guests who will attend the function.

## Observe/observed by (with)

***Observe*** means ***watch carefully.*** Please ***observe*** the behaviour of the students of this class. ***Observe by*** (with) is used in passive voice, ***means to occupy the mind with*** (fear or fixed ideas) or ***continually in distress.*** She ***observed*** with distress how people had suffered by the floods.

## Part/part with/parting

***Part*** means ***separate or divide.*** Let us ***part*** (leave) now. ***Part with*** means ***to give up*** or ***give away.*** I feel bad to

***part with*** my mother. Sheela hates to ***part with*** her money. ***Parting*** provides the meaning of ***departure***. Their ***parting*** early today left us with no company.

## Pass/pass it on/pass away/pass for/pass off/ pass on

It means ***move towards and beyond; proceed***. The path was so narrow that none could easily ***pass***. ***Pass on*** means ***to pass sentence on an accused person***; ***go unnoticed***. Her rude behaviour ***passed on*** without any resistance. ***Passed away*** means ***died***. She ***passed away*** a week earlier. ***Pass for*** means ***to be accepted***. The retired man who lives near by, is ***passed for*** (is taken to be) an intelligent man. ***Pass off*** means ***to take place***; ***be carried through.*** The meeting held last night in the President's chamber ***passed off*** peacefully. ***Pass on*** means ***die.*** The Health Minister ***passed on*** after a week's illness. ***Pass on*** also conveys ***to give or to deliver***. Please ***pass*** it ***on*** to the man standing on the footboard of the bus.

## Pay/pay back/pay off/ pay out

***Pay*** means ***wages*** or ***salary***. It means money ***paid for regular services or work***. His monthly ***pay*** is almost rupees ten thousand. ***Pay back*** means ***return that has been borrowed***. It also means ***to punish***. He ***paid*** me ***back*** the money, he had borrowed last month. She ***paid*** him ***back*** for what he did to her in life. It means she punished him for his atrocities or injustice done against her. ***Pay off*** means

***pay*** someone ***full to fulfil one's duty or obligation.*** The master ***paid off*** the servant at the end of the month. ***Paid out*** means ***give money in settlement of expenses.*** Past month's bills have been ***paid out*** in full.

## Pick/pick at/pick off/pick out/ pick over/pick up

It means ***to take up, remove, pull away with the fingers.*** Please ***pick*** some flowers from the garden. ***Pick at*** means ***find fault with.*** Please don't ***pick at*** your poor servant. ***Pick off*** means ***take*** or ***pluck off.*** The police ***picked off*** the culprit from the crowd. ***Pick out*** means ***to choose or distinguish from the surroundings***. Don't ***pick out*** red roses today for decorating the stage. ***Pick over*** means ***to examine and make a selection***. ***Pick over*** a basket of lilies only. ***Pick up*** means ***take and hold*** or ***lift***. Please ***pick up*** my hat from there.

## Play/play at/play down/play up/play with

***Play*** means ***to have fun*** or ***to pass the time pleasantly***. Little John is ***playing*** in the living room. Play at means to engage oneself half-heartedly. He is only playing at tennis. ***Play down*** means deliberately talk to or ***behave so that he/ she does not feel inferior to get support.*** Ramesh is ***playing down*** with the group so that they don't underrate him. ***Play up*** means to play vigorously or energetically. It also implies to behave mischievously. It seems that Harish has joined the club just to ***play up***. (Harish has joined the club just for some sort of mischief.) ***Play with*** means ***to consider lightly***. It is unfair on your part to ***play with*** your brother. It means that you are not treating your brother well and taking him lightly.

## Press/press up/press for/press on (upon)

***Press*** means ***to push steadily against***. Please ***press*** the bell hard so that it may ring well. ***Press up*** means ***physical exercise; stretching out***. Regular ***pressing up*** will help you shape your body well. ***Press for*** means ***to make repeated requests for*** or ***to insist on***. His mother is ***pressing*** him ***for*** going to gymnasium regularly. ***Press on*** means ***to oppress*** or ***weigh***. She was ***pressed on*** heavily on account of responsibilities after her father's death.

## Pull/pull together/pull on/pull about/pull apart/pull in/pull off/pull out/pull over/pull through/pull up

It means ***to use force upon so as to draw towards or after one***. She ***pulled*** the chair to sit on it. ***Pull together*** means ***work together***. All the workers are now ***pulling together***. ***Pull on*** means ***draw*** or ***suck***. He is ***pulling on*** his pipe. ***Pull about*** means ***treat roughly***; ***pull in different directions***. He has been ***pulling about*** as far the new plan is concerned. ***Pull apart*** means ***to tear into parts***. As she was so doleful, she tried to ***pull apart*** her hair. ***Pull in*** means ***to enter a station***. The train ***pulled in*** around 11 PM. ***Pull off*** gives the meaning of ***driving a motor***

***vehicle into a hard shoulder; succeed in a plan.*** We could ***pull off*** well as far as the last night programme is concerned. ***Pull out*** means ***move*** or ***row out.*** The current of the river was so strong that the boat ***pulled out*** into it by itself. ***Pull over*** means ***to steer to one side.*** Will you please ***pull over*** your car on the other side? ***Pull through*** means ***succeed in avoiding difficulties.*** The patient could finally ***pull through*** his illness. ***Pull up*** means to improve one's relative position. Meera could ***pull up*** in her studies a little before her examination.

## Put/put across/put aside/put away/put back/put down/put forth/put forward/put in/put out/put up

***Put*** means ***to move so as to be in a certain place***. He ***put*** the chair in the middle of the room. ***Put across*** means ***to communicate successfully***. He is a good teacher for he can ***put across*** his ideas to the students. ***Put aside*** means ***lay down*** or ***save***. She has ***put aside*** a good sum for the rainy days. ***Put away*** means ***put in the usual place of storage to save.*** She ***put*** her toys ***away***. ***Put back*** means ***return.*** She is a good librarian. She always ***puts back*** the books at the right place after the readers have used them. ***Put down*** means ***land***. She ***put*** her glider ***down*** at an unknown place. ***Put forth*** gives the sense of ***sending out***. The trees have ***put forth*** the new leaves after the autumn. ***Put forward*** means ***advance*** or ***to put before people for consideration***. Newton ***put forward*** a new theory before the world. ***Put***

***in (into)*** means ***enter.*** The big ship ***put in (into)*** the harbour after 24 hours. ***Put out*** means ***move out from the harbour*** or ***to extinguish***. Please ***put out*** the light. ***Put up*** means ***to obtain lodging and food for the night***. They ***put up*** in a lodge after midnight. ***Put up*** also means ***to make it known***. He will put up the matter in the meeting tomorrow.

## Reach/within reach/reach out /beyond reach (out of reach)

***Reach*** means ***stretch to reach.*** Expressions such as ***within reach/ reach out***, etc. are being projected with their uses only. That book is ***within*** my ***reach***. She ***reached out*** her hand to grab the book but it was too far to get. I like to keep my glasses ***within*** my ***reach*** so that when I need them I may ***reach*** (get) them. That ceiling fan is ***beyond (out of)*** my ***reach.***

## Reckon/ reckon in/reckon up/reckon with/ reckon on (upon)

***Reckon*** simply means ***to calculate***. I ***reckon*** the cost of this house should be so much. In this case, the meaning of ***reckon involves the sense of mental calculation***. ***Reckon in*** means ***include*** or ***take into account***. Did she ***reckon in*** all the cost of the house before selling it? ***Reckon up*** means ***to find the total of.*** Please ***reckon up*** the hotel bill properly. ***Reckon with*** means ***deal with; settle with***. We shall ***reckon with*** the contractor after the house is complete. ***Reckon on***

means ***depend on (upon)*** or ***base one's hopes on.*** She very much ***reckons on*** my help.

## Retire/retire from (to)/retired into (oneself)

It means ***withdraw*** or ***go away***. She ***retired*** (*from* the active service) at the age of fifty-two. He ***retired*** to his bedroom. In this case, the meaning of ***retired is that he went to sleep***. ***Retired into*** gives the sense ***to convey one's withdrawal from the social life***. ***She retired into*** herself. It means ***she became unsociable*** because she wrapped herself into her own thoughts. It's a kind of ***withdrawal from the world.***

## Ride/ride for a fall/ride in/ride on/ride out/ ride down

Its simple meaning is ***ride*** on a horse or sit on a bicycle, etc. and cause to go. He ***rides*** his horse everyday in the morning. ***Ride for a fall*** means ***riding recklessly***; ***riding for disaster. Ride in*** means ***be in and be carried in***. She will be ***riding in*** a bus around 5 o'clock. ***Ride on*** means ***sit*** or ***go or be on***. The child was ***riding on*** his father's shoulders. ***Ride out*** conveys the sense of ***coming safely through trouble***. We managed to ***ride out*** the storm. ***Ride down*** means ***chase on horseback and catch up with or to direct one's horse at someone and let the horse knock him down***. The police ***rode down*** fast and eventually, caught the culprit.

## Round/round off/round up/ round upon/ round about

***Round*** means ***go round.*** Don't ***go round*** that corner lest you should be hurt. ***Round off*** means ***bring it to a satisfactory conclusion***. He ***rounded off*** his career by becoming a police officer. ***Round up*** means ***bring it to a whole number***. The shopkeeper ***rounded up*** the price from Rupees 258 to Rupees 260. ***Round upon*** means ***to turn on and to attack***. She ***rounded upon*** the dog to frighten it. ***Round about*** means ***not going*** or ***coming by the shortest route***. They travelled by a ***round about*** way to reach Mumbai.

## Run/run across/run after/run against/run along/run away/run down/run into/run off with/ run on/ run out/run over

***Run*** means to move with a quick speed. She ***ran*** fast to catch the train. ***Run across*** means ***pay a short informal visit***. I ***ran across*** to my brother's house to borrow a book. ***Run after*** means ***try to catch***. The cat was ***running after*** a mouse. ***Run against*** mean to ***compete with someone by running in a race***. Heera Lal ***ran against*** his opponent in the last election with great fortitude. ***Run along*** means ***to go away*** or ***be off.*** Better ***run along*** now. ***Run away*** means ***leave rapidly*** or ***to flee***. The thieves ***ran away*** as soon they heard some noise in the house. ***Run down*** means ***to stop because something*** or ***someone has become weak***

or ***exhausted***. The clock on the wall has ***run down. Run into*** gives the sense of ***meeting someone unexpectedly***. A very old friend of mine ***ran*** into me in the street nearby. ***Run off with*** means ***to steal and take away***. The accountant has ***run off with*** all the important documents of the company. ***Run on*** means ***to talk continuously.*** Can you stop for a moment as you have been ***running on*** for a very long time? ***Run out*** gives the sense of ***going out*** or ***come to an end***. The provisions in the house are ***running out. Run over*** means ***review or recapitulate***. Let us ***run over*** the course again to develop more confidence.

## Save/save from/save face/save up (for)

***Save*** means ***make or keep safe from loss, injury, etc***. A good doctor will always help ***saving*** his patient. ***Save from*** is used in a similar sense ***to express keeping safe from injury*** or ***danger or getting damaged, etc***. Please ***save*** Shyam ***from*** drowning, as he does not know swimming well. ***Save face*** is used to convey when ***one avoids the risk of loss*** or ***injury, etc***. He often ***saves*** his ***face*** when encountered with problems. ***Save up*** means ***to keep for future***. We should always ***save up (for)*** some provisions for the next day or future. You should always ***save*** enough ***for*** your children.

## Scrape/scrape from (off)/ scrape out/scrape through/ scrape together

***Scrape*** means ***to make smooth or level by pushing the hard edge of a tool along the surface. Scrape from*** means ***to remove mud, grease, etc in this way***. Please ***scrape*** the dirt ***from*** the floor of the living room at once. ***Scrape out*** means ***making by scraping. Scrape out*** dirt from the windowpanes properly. ***Scrape through*** means ***just passed.*** Her son just ***scraped through*** the examination. ***Scrape together*** means ***to obtain by being careful*** or ***with effort.*** The police managed ***to scrape together*** some crowd when the minister was about to deliver his talk.

## Search/search out/ search for

***Search*** means ***to examine; look carefully at, through*** or ***into***. She ***searched*** her room thoroughly but she could not find her ring. ***Search out*** means ***look for*** or ***examine carefully.*** Please ***search out*** your own conscience carefully before you pass judgement on others. ***Search for*** means ***to find out*** or ***to discover***. I am trying to ***search for*** the lost article since morning.

## See/see about/see across/see around/see back/see off/see over/see through

***See*** means to ***use the power of sight***. I cannot ***see*** through this small hole in the night. ***See about*** means ***deal with.*** She assured me that she would ***see about*** the matter. ***See across*** means ***guide, to conduct, to help it across***. Please help the boy to ***see across*** the road for he cannot see properly. ***See around*** means ***to say good bye***. We shall like to ***see*** her ***around. See back*** means ***to accompany***. It is quite late in the night. ***See off*** is used when ***one departs and is seen off at the railway station, airport or bus stand.*** I am going to the airport to ***see off*** my brother who is going by the 5 o 'clock flight. ***See over*** means ***to visit and examine***. I shall ***see over*** the house that you intend to buy. ***See through*** means ***not to be deceived by***. I could easily ***see through*** him and understood his dirty tricks.

## Sell/sell to/sell off/sell out/sell up

***Sell*** means ***give in exchange of money***. I ***sold*** my goods at a good price. ***Sell to*** is used like "I shall ***sell*** it ***to*** you when you are ready to buy it." ***Sell off*** indicates ***selling cheaply***. I shall ***sell*** the fruits ***off*** so that all are sold by the evening. ***Sell out*** is used ***to indicate part*** or ***all of one's share in a business***. She ***sold out*** all her shares to another company with a great profit. ***Sell up*** is used ***when someone pays for his debts***. When he lost most of his property in gambling, he ***sold up*** his assets to *pay off* his debts.

## Send/send away/send down/ send for/send in/send off/send on/send out

***Send*** means ***cause to go*** or ***be carried without going***. Please ***send*** him to me. You should ***send*** it by post. ***Send away*** means ***to dismiss*** or ***order from a distance***. At times, we need to ***send away*** for many things that we don't get in our town. ***Send down*** means ***to expel a student from a university for misconduct.*** It also provides the meaning of ***causing to fall.*** The bumper crop of wheat ***sent*** its price ***down.*** Satish was ***sent down*** from the college on account of his misconduct in the class. ***Send for*** means ***to ask or order to come.*** Please don't remove anything from this room until I ***send for*** someone to do so. ***Send in*** means ***to send for some competition*** or ***exhibition.*** Please don't forget to ***send in*** two names for the coming competition. ***Send off*** means ***to go with someone to a place where from he/she will start the journey.*** We all went to the railway station to give her a hearty ***send off.*** ***Send on*** means ***to send in advance.*** She asked me to ***send*** her letters ***on*** while she was away from the town. ***Send out*** means ***to distribute*** or ***to give out.*** These trees ***send out*** new leaves after autumn.

## Serve/serve on/serve out/ serve with/serve for

It means ***be a servant to*** or ***work for.*** He ***served*** me for ten years. ***Serve on*** means be a member of. I ***served on*** the various committees of the university for several years. ***Serve out*** means ***attend to customers in a shop.*** Food was ***served out*** to the flood victims, twice in a day. ***Serve with*** gives almost the same sense as ***serve out.*** These days most of our villages are ***served with*** electricity and water. ***Serve for*** provides the meaning of ***serving satisfactorily for a need or purpose.*** This book will ***serve for*** me. It means that the particular book will help him/her in examination or to get knowledge.

## Set/set about/set against/set apart/set back /set down/set forth/set off/set on/set out

It means ***to move or place so as to reach it. Set about means to start or take steps towards*** a certain place or a thing. She ***set about*** her friend heavily. It means she started fighting with him. ***Set against*** means ***to struggle against or cause to compete with***. The President of the Club ***set*** the members ***against*** each other. ***Set apart*** means to put on one side for future use. Don't keep any malice within. ***Set*** personal feelings ***apart*** and become friends once again. ***Set back*** means move back. Please ***set*** the hands of the clock ***back*** to correct the time. ***Set down*** means ***put down (allow to get down or to get out)***. The car stopped to ***set down*** one person. ***Set forth*** means ***began a journey or make known*** or ***declare***. You must ***set forth*** your political ambitions clearly. ***Set off*** means ***to start a race*** or ***journey***. She has ***set off*** for Delhi. ***Set on*** means ***go forward*** or ***attack.*** He was ***set on*** by a mad dog last night. ***Set out*** means ***begin a journey***. She ***set out*** with a heavy heart.

## Settle/settle down/settle for/settle on/ settle with

***Settle*** means ***to establish***. He is ***settled*** in London. ***Settle down*** means ***to sit*** or ***lie comfortably***. She ***settled down*** in her study to read seriously. ***Settle for*** means ***to accept but***

***not quite satisfactorily***. When I sold my car, I had ***to settle for*** a price that was not quite suitable for me. ***Settle on*** means ***to give for use during one's lifetime***. It also ***means to decide***. I have decided to ***settle on*** part of my property on my eldest son. Which of the two books you like ***to settle on. Settle with*** means ***to pay what one owes to.*** She says that she will ***settle with*** us on the last day of the month.

## Shake/shake down/shake off/shake out/shake it out/shake it up

***Shake*** means ***cause to move from side to side, up and down***. He ***shook*** her by the shoulder. ***Shake down*** means ***become adjusted to*** or ***get into harmony in a new environment*** or ***new conditions***. Our new servant is ***shaking down*** admirably. ***Shake off*** means ***to free oneself from***. Please don't get depressed and ***shake*** yourself ***off*** from it. ***Shake out*** means ***to spread*** or ***disperse***. The boys were ordered ***to shake out*** as soon as they came out of the class. ***Shake it out*** gives the sense of ***to be out by shaking***. Please ***shake*** the fruits ***out*** from the tree. ***Shake it up*** means ***mix it up by shaking***. Please ***shake up*** the glass of the juice before you drink it.

## Shut/shut down/shut in/shut off/shut out/shut up

***Shut*** means ***move into position to stop an opening.*** Please ***shut*** the door soon lest the dust should enter it. ***Shut down*** means ***stop working; end activity***. The clinic has

***shut down*** and its workers are now unemployed. ***Shut in*** provides the meaning of ***closing or confining***. The prisoner is ***shut in*** a small cell for the whole night. ***Shut off*** means ***stop the supply*** or ***flow of***. The landlord of the house has ***shut off*** the supply of electricity and we are in great difficulty, right now. ***Shut out*** means ***to keep out*** or ***to exclude***. Please don't ***shut*** me ***out*** of your company. ***Shut up*** means to close and secure all the doors and windows. It seems that the storm is about to come, so ***shut up*** all the windows and the doors immediately. ***Shut up*** also means ***to keep quiet and stop talking***. ***Shut up***. Will you?

## Stand/stand aside/stand back/stand by/stand down/stand for/stand in/stand off/stand out/ stand over/stand to/stand up/stand with

***Stand*** means ***stopping of motion and progress. Stop*** the bus right now. ***Stand aside*** means ***to be inactive and do nothing***. Why do you ***stand aside*** when you need to be actively working? ***Stand back*** means ***move back***. The policeman ***stood back*** when the accident occurred in front of his eyes. ***Stand by*** means to ***be a bystander*** or ***look on without doing anything***. You should not ***stand by*** when I am grabbed with odd circumstances. ***Stand down*** means ***retire from a witness box*** or ***similar position***. My neighbour, who was contesting election for the position of Municipal Commissioner, has ***stood down*** in favour of his friend. ***Stand for*** means ***to represent***. Who will ***stand for***

you in the next meeting when you are away from here? ***Stand in*** provides the meaning of ***taking a share in***. Let us ***stand in*** for you if the expenses of the party are so high. ***Stand off*** means ***to remain at a distance*** or ***move away***. Please ***stand off*** from here until all the mines are blasted. ***Stand out*** means ***to be easily seen above*** or ***among others***. If you work hard, it will ***stand out*** from that of others. ***Stand over*** means ***to be postponed***. Let these ideas ***stand over*** until we don't think anything better than that. ***Stand to*** means ***to take up a position to resist a possible attack***. She ***stood to*** for a long time to repel any retort against her. ***Stand up*** means ***to stand upright***. He likes to eat his lunch while ***standing up***. ***Stand with*** means ***to be on (good) terms with*** or ***be well thought of***. Our new boss seems to be a good person. He ***stands with*** all the employees.

## Step/ step aside/step down/step in/step off (out)/ step up

***Step*** means ***move one foot after the other—forward*** or ***in the direction indicated***. Please ***step*** into the next room and see how beautifully it has been decorated. ***Step aside*** means ***move to one side***. Would you mind to ***step aside*** so that I can also sit well? ***Step down*** means ***to resign***. The old boss ***stepped down*** and the new one joined in his place on the next day. ***Step in*** means ***to intervene***. If you had not ***stepped in***, the case would have been totally spoiled. ***Step off (out)*** means ***to measure by taking steps***. Please ***step out (off)*** five metres from this point. ***Step up*** means

***to fix or increase***. Please ***step up*** your efforts to complete the project on time.

## Strike/strike down/strike off/strike on (upon)/strike through/strike up

***Strike*** means ***to hit; to give a blow***. She ***struck*** the table with her fist several times. ***Strike down*** means to ***hit one so that one falls to the ground***. ***Strike off*** means ***cut off with a blow*** or ***to remove***. The teacher ***struck off*** Hari's name from the attendance register. ***Strike on (upon)*** conveys the meaning of ***getting or finding suddenly or unexpectedly.*** An idea ***struck on*** her mind all of a sudden. ***Strike through*** means ***cross out*** or ***to put a line*** or ***lines through***. The examiner ***struck through*** the answer book as he thought that the student had cheated. ***Strike up*** means ***begin to play***. He ***struck up*** an acquaintance with a fellow passenger during his journey to Srinagar.

## Take/take back/take after/take apart (from)/take down/take into account/take off/ take out/take over/take to/take up/ take upon

***Take*** means ***get*** or ***lay hold of with the hands or any other part of the body. Please take this letter and post it today***. ***Take back*** means ***retreat*** or ***withdraw as an admission of error.*** It also provides the sense ***of bringing back the old memories to one's mind.*** My friend will not ***take back*** the gift, he gave me yesterday. I don't like that gift so I wish to return it to him. ***Take after*** means ***to resemble in features*** or ***character.*** His son ***takes after*** him to a great extent. ***Take apart (from)*** means ***to separate into its parts.*** Please ***take*** this electrical part ***apart*** to locate fault in it. Please ***take*** this electrical part ***apart from*** its main body to locate fault in it. ***Take down*** means ***write down***. The students ***took down*** the teacher's entire lecture in the class. ***Take into account*** means ***to take into confidence***. My new clerk is a trustworthy person. You can ***take*** him ***into account***. ***Take off*** gives the sense of ***making a start in jumping.*** The flight ***took off*** right at 10 A.M. ***Take out*** means ***to extract*** or ***to remove***. Can she ***take out*** the dirty spots from my shirt? ***Take over*** provides the meaning ***to carry from one place to another.*** He ***took*** me ***over*** to the park in his car. ***Take to*** means ***to adopt as a practice or hobby or as a means of livelihood***. I shall ***take*** to photography ***after*** my retirement. ***Take up*** provides the sense of ***lifting up*** or ***rising***. She ***took up*** the story at the point I had left it yesterday. ***Take upon*** means ***to assume responsibility***. He must ***take upon*** himself the right to make decisions about his daughter's further schooling.

## Tear/tear away (from)/torn between

***Tear*** means ***to pull sharply apart*** or ***to pieces***. Please ***tear*** this piece of paper properly. ***Tear away*** means ***to leave*** or ***to stop doing it***. He could hardly tear himself ***away*** *from* the sad feeling. ***Torn between*** means ***painfully distracted by having to choose between conflicting demands, desires***

or ***decisions.*** She was ***torn between*** the diverse opinions of her husband and her father, as both did not seem to be coming to any conclusion regarding the particular situation.

## Think/think about/think of/think highly of /think well/think little/think it out/think over/think up

***Think*** means ***use*** or ***exercise the mind in order to form opinions*** or ***come to conclusion***. I ***think*** he is right in this matter. ***Think about*** means ***to examine*** or ***consider (a plan or idea whether it is desirable).*** When I ***think about*** your conduct I feel bad as you often react against when you ought not to. ***Think of*** means ***to consider; take into account.*** Better ***think of*** every aspect of the problem before coming to any conclusion. ***Think highly of*** means ***to have a high, good opinion of.*** She thinks ***highly of you. Think well*** means ***think good of someone***. He always ***thinks well*** of her. ***Think little*** means not to think much about someone; ***not quite significant***. I ***think little*** of him, as he does not appeal to me much. ***Think it out*** means ***consider carefully and make a plan for.*** Your plan to purchase a new house seems good but ***think it out*** once again before you execute the plan. ***Think over*** means ***to reflect upon; consider further***. I advise you ***to think it over*** before making a decision. ***Think up*** means ***to devise, conceive or invent***. We really don't know what she will ***think up*** next.

## Throw/throw about/throw oneself/throw away/throw back on (upon)/throw oneself down/throw in/ throw it off

***Throw*** means cause ***to go through the air***. She ***throws*** quite well. Ask the children not to ***throw*** stones. ***Throw about*** means ***to scatter***. Please don't ***throw about*** the foodstuff on the dining table. ***Throw oneself*** means ***to rush violently at***. Please don't ***throw yourself*** at the people in the restaurant. ***Throw away*** mean***s lose by foolishness or neglect.*** Her efforts to mend him were ***thrown away*** (wasted). ***Throw back on*** means ***show characteristics of, revert to.*** When he failed to appear to bring his car to carry us to Delhi, we were ***thrown back on*** to drive our old car. ***Throw oneself down*** means ***lie down at full length.*** She ***threw herself down*** in front of her *guru* as she revered him most. ***Throw in*** means ***to supply extra without an addition to the price.*** We are selling fruits today at a ***throw in*** price. ***Throw it off*** means ***to manage to get rid off, become free from.*** She possesses a poetic temperament that she can ***throw a new poem off*** any time.

## Tie/tie it down/tie in with/tie it up/tie it on/ tie with (for)

***Tie*** means ***fasten or bind with a string or rope, etc***. Please ***tie*** these branches of the tree together. ***Tie it down*** means ***to restrict freedom***. Please ***tie the thief down*** until the police come. ***Tie in with*** means ***to link or be linked with.***

These two stories don't seem to be ***tied in with*** each other. ***Tie it up*** means ***to invest (capital) so that it is not easily available.*** Please ***tie up your property*** in such a manner that none could sell it without your permission. ***Tie it on*** means ***to fasten by means of strings. Please tie the label on*** the bottle properly so that it does not get away. ***Tie with (for)*** means ***equal in points (in games).*** These two basketball teams ***tied with*** each other in the finals.

## Tire/tire out/ be tired of

***Tire*** means ***to make or become weary***. I am ***tired*** so I need rest. ***Tire out*** means ***in need of rest or uninterested.*** I was ***tired out*** by a long walk. ***Be tired of*** means ***to have had enough of*** or ***be exhausted with***. She seems to ***be tired of*** with eating rice in lunch everyday. Actually, ***tired of*** is quite a common expression to convey one's anger by saying, ***I am tired of you***, ***which simply means I don't like you*** or ***I am disgusted with you***.

## Touch/touch at/touch down/touch it for/ touch it off/touch on (upon)/ touch it up

***Touch*** means ***to be in contact with***. Please keep in ***touch*** with me when you have gone out. ***Touch at*** means ***to call at*** or ***to reach at***. The boat ***touched at*** the shore early in the morning. ***Touch down*** means ***to come down to land***. The plane ***touched down*** the runway very smoothly. ***Touch it for*** means ***to get money from (begging).*** She ***touched me for*** ten rupees. ***Touch it off*** means ***to discharge or cause to***

***start***. During the country's independence when great leaders were arrested, it ***touched off*** a great disturbance among the people. ***Touch on (upon)*** means ***treat briefly.*** When I arrived at their daughter's wedding, they simply ***touched*** me ***on***. ***Touch it up*** means ***to make small changes in a picture or a piece of writing or is used when dressing up–to improve it.*** You need ***to touch this essay up*** once again.

## Try/try for/try on/try out

***Try*** means ***to make an attempt***. She ***tried*** very hard to win the race. ***Try for*** means ***to make an attempt to get or win.*** He ***tried for*** it wholeheartedly and finally got it. ***Try on*** means ***to put on garments to see whether it fits or looks well.*** The tailor asked him to ***try on*** his new trousers to assure him that it was done well. ***Try out*** means ***to use it; to experiment with it.*** Though your plan seems to be well, still it needs to be ***tried out.***

## Turn/turn about/turn adrift/turn against/ turn aside (from)/turn away/ turn back/ turn down/turn off/turn on/turn out/turn over/turn round/turn to

***Turn*** means ***to move round a point***. She ***turned*** towards me to listen to what I had been telling others. ***Turned about*** means ***cause to turn to one side or in a different direction***. Please ***turn about*** to see a beautiful sight of the nature. ***Turn adrift*** means ***to send away without help*** or

***support.*** He ***turned*** his father ***adrift*** in the world. (It means sent him away from home without any sort of help). ***Turn against*** means ***to become hostile to***. She tried ***to turn*** the children ***against*** her husband. ***Turn aside*** means ***cause to turn to one side*** or ***in a different direction***. After listening to my explanation, she ***turned aside*** instantly. ***Turn away*** means ***cause to turn in a different direction so as not to face; refuse to look at.*** He ***turned away*** from me when I implored him to help me. ***Turn back*** means ***to return the way one has come***. Since the sun was in the west, darkness prevailed. Therefore, we all ***turned back*** home. ***Turn down*** is mostly used ***to show one's refusal to consider something.*** The company offered him a good job but he ***turned it down*** for reasons best known to him. ***Turn off*** provides the meaning of ***changing the direction*** or ***stopping the flow of gas, current, etc.*** Please ***turn off*** the light. The music is so boring that it has ***turned*** my mood ***off. Turn on*** means ***start the flow of liquid, etc. Turn on*** the gas immediately. ***Turn out*** means ***to prove to be; be in the end.*** At the end, all ***turned out*** well. ***Turn over*** means ***cause to fall over; to upset*** or ***change the position of.*** She ***turned over*** in the bed. The doctor ***turned over*** the patient to give him some pills. ***Turn round*** means ***to face another way*** or ***be in another direction***. She ***turned*** her chair ***round*** to the fire to enjoy its warmth. ***Turn to*** means ***to get busy.*** The printing staff ***turned to*** and printed the entire book in one night.

## Wait/wait for/wait up/wait on (upon)

***Wait*** means ***to stay where one is or delay acting until it comes***. Please ***wait*** a few seconds and I shall be ready. ***Wait for*** is also used in similar situations. Can you ***wait for*** me at the railway station? ***Wait up*** conveys the sense ***to stay up and not to go to bed***. Could you kindly ***wait up*** until I finish this article? ***Wait on (upon)*** means ***to act as a servant to, fetch and carry things for.*** Most husbands want their wives ***to wait on (upon)*** them.

## Walk/walk about/walk away from/walk away with/walk off with/walk into/walk out/walk over

***Walk*** means ***to move both feet off the ground at once***. She is much better now and can ***walk*** at least a mile. ***Walk about*** means ***a journey; conveys the sense of meeting people informally by a celebrity.*** I like to ***walk about*** occasionally. When our Prime Minister comes to our town, he often likes to ***walk about*** to have a casual acquaintance with the people. ***Walk away from*** means ***beat easily in a contest.*** Sheela ***walked away*** from all her mates in a hundred-metre race run in her college. ***Walk away with*** means ***to win easily; carry off; take.*** Padukar ***walked away with*** in the badminton finals in England, several years ago. ***Walked off with*** means ***carry off*** or ***take***. He ***walked off with*** my wristwatch. ***Walked into*** means ***eat heartily of; abuse or scold; meet with someone suddenly*** or ***barge in.*** She ***walked***

***into*** the rice-pudding. (It means she ate the rice pudding heartily) I actually did not know that they were indulging in a quarrel. I just ***walked into*** it. ***Walked out*** means ***to go on strike***. The workers of this factory have just ***walked out. Walked over*** means ***to defeat one easily; easy victory without or a little contest.*** I got a ***walk over*** in the tennis match that I was to play last night.

## Wipe/wipe away/wipe off/wipe out/wipe up

***Wipe*** means ***to clean or dry by rubbing with a cloth, paper, etc***. Please ***wipe*** your hand with this towel. ***Wipe away*** means to remove by wiping. Please try hard to ***wipe away*** the stain from my shirt. ***Wipe off*** also means ***to remove by wiping***. Please ***wipe off*** the blackboard properly. ***Wipe out*** means ***to clean the inside of; get rid of; remove***. You must learn to ***wipe out*** old quarrels. ***Wipe up*** means ***to take up (liquid, etc.) by wiping.*** Please ***wipe up*** the spilt milk from the floor.

# Dialogues/ Short and Long Conversation

The example of dialogues/conversation given below, are simply guidelines to initiate or to carry on a talk. The reader may develop or begin conversation in any way but if he/she uses common words to convey varied sorts of meanings, it would certainly enrich the conversation and fascinate the talk. Some examples are given below:

**1**

Meena : Good Morning, Mrs. Smiles. Did you receive my letter sent to you last week?

Mrs. Smiles : Yes, I did.?

Meena : Why didn't you *acknowledge* it? I had been worrying for you so much.

Mrs. Smiles : I am sorry not to reply it soon. But I was not sure of your *address*, as you had simply scribbled it.

Meena : But you could have paid some attention to my *appeal to* visit me next month. If my address was not clearly written in the letter, you could phone me.

Mrs. Smiles : Oh! I am awfully sorry. I just forgot that I had your phone number too.
In future, I shall not repeat this mistake. *By the way*, could you please tell me your full address now?

**2**

Sheela : Hai, Seema! How are you?

Seema : Oh, Sheela, I am fine. When did you come to Delhi? How are things?

Sheela : I came to Delhi last week. I am fine. I need to *arrange for* a car for my brother who wants to go to Chandigarh next week. Do you know any car dealer?

Seema : Yes, I do. One of my cousins is running a taxi-stand. He has around four taxies. I will give his telephone number. Please contact him soon. He will solve your problem.

Sheela : Thank you Seema. You have solved my problem.

**3**

John : Hai, Bunty, how are you doing?

Bunty : I am pretty good. What about the plan I submitted to you last week?

John : The plan seems to be good. But I haven't yet *approved of* it.

Bunty : Why didn't you approve of it so far?

John : Well, I have not seriously seen it. I shall try *to go through* ( read) it today and then approve it if I find it good.

**4**

Deepak : (While talking to his senior) Sir, The CEO was highly disturbed to read the report. He *blew it out* with rage and hurdled an *avalanche of* words in the meeting.

Mr. Kumar : Oh yes! What a way of expressing wrath! I feel that he talks like a *babbler* whenever he is in rage.

Deepak : Yes sir, he often *bears grudge against* the people who don't hesitate to tell the truth.

Mr. Kumar : By the way, why was the CEO angry with the workers?

Deepak : They simply requested him to increase their wages. That *made him mad.*

**5**

Kareem : Salma, you seem to be very restless today. Why don't you sit *beside* me and tell me your problems.

Salma : I would like to share my problems with you, as you are my friend.

*Besides*, you are also my cousin so I shall tell you all what happened with me in the party.

Kareem : You are much *better* than other women. The *better* I know you, the more I understand you.

Salma : I *admit* you have a good sense of understanding. Let me tell you the truth. It was not my fault to walk *across* the floor. As there was no room for me to sit on this side of the room, so I *walked on* to the other side. I also didn't *notice* (see/observe) that Sharif had kept a seat for me *beside* him. What an embarrassing situation! He went on shouting at me as I took a seat on the other side. You can't stop creating a scene at times without knowing its consequences.

**6**

Sam : Peter, don't feel disturbed on account of hard days. All will be well soon. Please don't *abandon* your duty towards the children. It is not wise to *abandon yourself to* despair when surrounded with *dismal* situations.

Peter : Sam I am so disheartened these days, I really *acknowledge*.

Sam : Why are you not regular to your work? What *affairs* are keeping you busy other than your routine duty.

Peter : I can't describe how sick is my wife these days! I cannot *bar* my thoughts to think of her *as* she is so dear to me.

Sam : I really appreciate and *acknowledge* your concern towards your wife. But who will look after the children if you *abandon* their care? Please take my advice. Do *look after* your wife but I *appeal to* you to give equal attention towards the children as well.

Peter : Yes, you are right. I had forgotten my duty towards my children. How can I *abandon* them? I love them so dearly. I shall take care of everything, you have mentioned.

7

Suraj : Where are your going, Mohan?

Mohan : I am intending to go to Pune.

Suraj : But the train you have *boarded* is *bound for* Mumbai.

Mohan : Yes, I know it. First I shall go to Mumbai where I intend to stay for a week.Then I shall proceed to Pune. Have you *been* to Pune, Suraj?

Suraj : No, I have never seen Pune. It must be a beautiful city.

Mohan : It is not only beautiful but cool also. During summer, you can live there very comfortably, *as* the temperature is always moderate there.

**8**

Satish : Why at all you want to *break away* with me?

Kapil : I really cannot *bear* you *for long* on account of your disposition.

Satish : What is wrong with my nature? It is you who often *break out* in anger and try to abuse our relationship.

Kapil : Well, if you don't like me, I can *break away* with you finally.

Satish : How can you think of *breaking away* from me? Even if you do so, I shall *break through* that situation and try to *make up* once again.

Kapil : I really don't understand you at times. If you behave like that, I shall change my opinion for you. Hope you don't give me any chance to think differently for you in future.

**9**

Mathew : Wilson, Why did you *break away* with Sophia without any cause?

Wilson : Mathew, you know that last month I was surrounded by great problems.

It was *but* for your help that I was almost ruined. It was Sophia who promised *to stand by* me under difficult circumstances, but she just did not. Though she is a nice person *but* not very trustworthy. So I had no other way left *but* to *abandon* her company.

Mathew : If I were you, I would give her one more chance. I reckon you need to cool down and don't *abandon* her without understanding her circumstances.

**10**

Saleem : What are your plans for today, Rafeek?

Rafeek : I don't have any plans to take *care of* right now. But I am busy day after.

I always like to *care about* my plans. Would you *care to* go for a walk right now to discuss the plan which I *care about* a lot?

Saleem : I would love to discuss it with you but right now, I don't *care for* a walk.

Hope you don't mind it.

Rafeek : Oh yes! Don't worry! But could you spare sometime tomorrow for me to take *care of* it?

Saleem : Surely I would.

## 11

Hakim : Pradeep, do you *carry* any boxes to the railway station tonight?

Mandira : *Intercepts.* No, Pradeep does not *carry* any load with him but he always *carries* a small suitcase with him. I reckon he will *carry* it unto his last journey.

Pradeep : I think Mandira is kidding. Yes, I often *carry* it with me, as it is not only handy but has also *carried* me *through* in difficulties. When once I lost my luggage while travelling from France to India, what I had was my suitcase that *carried* my clothes and money. It helped me a lot.

Mandira : Oh! That makes you *carry* it mostly with you.

Pradeep : Yes, you are right.

## 12

Mohan : Where is the *case* to keep my jewellery?

Daleep : How would I know where is it? *In case,* you had given it to me, I would have remembered it well.

Mohan : Daleep, I am not blaming you for it, for you often forget what I say to you. But just *in case* you find it, please let me know.

Daleep : Please do not forget to set the fire alarm!

Just *in case of* fire, see that the alarm goes on.

Mohan : Well, I don't think we need to set the fire alarm. There is hardly any chance of fire breaking out tonight. Besides, we all are awake until late in the night. It seems to me that you are too much scared of it without any cause.

**13**

Deepika : Tendulker took a fine *catch* in the second innings, isn't it?

Pushpa : Yes he did, but did you notice that Saleem was *caught* napping?

Deepika : Yes, you are right. Hey, what about Yuvraj?

Pushpa : I don't quite catch your meaning. What did happen to him?

Deepika : Yuvraj was talking to the wicket keeper when he had a *chance* to *take* a *catch.* But he could not.

Pushpa : Well, it seems that our players, though good, don't take things seriously.

**14**

Prakash : Can you *change* your clothes? They look so hopeless.

Jaideep : I shall do it if you so like. It will take me five minutes to *change*.

Prakash : Jaideep, can you go to market *to change* this $20 bill into Indian rupees?

Jaideep : Will you please *change over* your habit of bossing on others? You often annoy me by your nature. I would very much like you to *change to* a new way of thinking. You still believe in the old customs, which have no importance today.

Prakash : Yes, I will think about it. But could you think of *changing* the old house and buy a new one? It will give you a great *change for* the better.

Perhaps, it will also improve your way of living.

**15**

Doctor : Who is *in charge* in the night shift?

Matron : Sir, Sister Sheeva has that *charge*. Do you want me to call her if you want to give her some new instructions?

Doctor : Yes, *better* call her. I want her to be *in charge* of the bed thirteen as well in the next ward. That patient's condition is too precarious.

Matron : Sir, Sister Sheeva in already *in charge of* a full ward. It will be difficult for her to be in *charge of* another bed in the next ward.

## 16

Peter : Did you properly *check in* the hotel? Did you *check* that our luggage was put in the trolley properly?

Tom : Yes I did. But I forgot to note the *check out* time.

Peter : Please keep a *check upon* your memory. Lest you should forget your own name! (*Laughs loudly*)

Tom : What do you mean? Better you *check* your own luggage before blaming me for any lost articles.

Peter : Yes I will do it, but why don't you check the entire luggage at once so that nothing is lost by us?

## 17

Satish : Roma, better you *clean* your hands before serving food. Put some *clean* towels in the bath at the washbasin and give me a *clean* sheet of paper.

Heera : Yes, I will do. Did you hear about Jack's case?

Satish : No, I did not. What about Jack? What happened to him?

Heera : Jack is involved in a murder case. The police are after him. He says that he has done nothing and he is *clean* in that case. So far, Jack has a *clean* record.

Satish : What made the police think that Jack is not *clean*? Do you know that Jack is a great gambler?

Heera : No, I really don't know that. How do you know all that about him?

Satish : Once I had a chance to play cards with him in the club. He is so clever at cards that he *cleaned* me *out* in a few minutes.

Heera : What a surprise! So far, I never knew that Jack is a gambler too. Well, let the Lord save him then!

**18**

Prakash : The sky seems to be *clear* tonight. There is no *chance* for rain.

Neera : Yes, it looks like that. But are you very *clear about* it? At times, it rains without any notice. (*Neera says something in an undertone.*)

Prakash : What did you say? I am not *clear* what you said.

Neera : I simply said, "What makes you possess such *clear cut* ideas about the rain not falling tonight?"

Prakash : I said so as I am so *clear about* certain things.

I can say so by looking at the sky. Better sleep *clear of* the windows tonight.

Neera : Why should we stay *clear of* the windows when you are certain that it may not rain tonight?

Prakash : You never know God's ways. It may rain without any signs of it in advance.

**19**

Seema : Ritika, you are standing too *close* to me as if you are posing for a *close up*. Will you mind to move a little on the other side?

Ritika : I don't like such comments but surely, I am keeping a *close watch* on you. Therefore, I am standing so *close* to you. If you don't like it, I can stand *close behind* you. The play is about *to close* and there is no pleasure for me to stay so *close to* you. Just *close* your eyes and you will find me far away from you.

Seema : Please, don't say like that. How can I *close* my eyes when you are so *close to* me? Moreover, you also live *close* to me. I do like your company but I don't want to hurt you by my comments. Well, let us come to the point. Don't you think that the play is about to *close down*?

Ritika : Yes, you are right. It is time for the play to *close down*. Let us *clear out* from here a little early so that we can avoid the rush.

**20**

Natasha : Who is in *control* of this house? It seems all in disorder. Are there many children in this house? The furniture and books are scattered. It is better to keep *control* on children so they don't make the house so dirty.

Neera : Please keep *control over* your anger. It happens at times that children like to play as they like. It is not easy *to control* them all the time.

Natasha : It is true that children cannot be *controlled* all the time but someone should keep *control over* them to make them learn discipline.

Neera : I don't like children to be *controlled* at such an early age. Let them enjoy their childhood and play as they like. It is the way to make them grow well.

**21**

Mohan : Preetam, why are you sitting under the tree?

Preetam : I am just sitting under the shade of the tree to keep *cool*. It also helps you to *cool down* when you sit under such a shade. Besides, sitting under the shade of a tree also does not *cost* you anything.

Mohan : In the *course of* my life, I have never tried to sit under the shade of a tree.

Preetam : How I wish you had tried it. It would neither cost you anything nor it would tax you in anyway. Rather, it would provide you an unusual calmness that would keep you *cool headed* for long in the *course of* your life.

Mohan : Thank you for your kind advice. I shall try it at *all cost* now.

I am sure in *due course of* time, I shall learn the benefits of sitting under a shade and become *cool.* At least, it will keep me *cool* and help me *to choose* the right track onwards. There is no use *crying* for things that are not important. One must learn it as early as possible in the *course of* one's life.

**22**

Silva : Jack, why did you *cry off* at the last moment when you had promised to help John in his adversity?

Jack : There is always some reason to do that. I did so *as* John *denied* to *acknowledge* his mistake.

Silva : What was his mistake? Can you please speak it out?

Jack : Well, it is a different kind of mistake. Anyway, I shall tell you that if you so insist.

Silva : I shall be more than happy to learn what John did which made you *cry off* at the last moment.

Jack : Silva, you don't know the truth. He *deserted* Neena without any reason. You know that very well that Neena is my real sister. I really don't know what *designs* he had in mind, but he left Neena in the lurch without any cause.

Silva : Let us call John and ask him what made him *desert* such a good girl like Neena. (*John is summoned*)

Silva : John, please tell us the truth. Why have you *dropped off* visiting Neena these days? What *designs* have *directed* you to *desert* Neena?

John : Silva, it is not true that I have any *designs* to *desert* Neena. I still love her. It is simply on account of *ups and downs* in life that have made my visits *drop off* at Neena's. I am waiting for a good opportunity that I shall propose to her and soon we will marry.

Silva : Jack, what do you say now? Do you accept what John has said right now?

Jack : Well, if it is the *case,* I am so happy. I shall *stand* once again *to* help him if he needs it.

**23**

Master : Bholu, Stand *at ease*, and reply my questions carefully.

Bholu : Sir, how can I be *at ease*, unless you try to listen what I say?

Master : OK. Go ahead. I can *ease off* your problems if you tell me everything correctly. Don't ask *excuses* for nothing. I simply want you to tell me the truth *face to face* so that I know who is at fault. Don't ask any *excuses for* the wrong things, you have done.

Bholu : Why would I *ask for* any *excuses*? I am not that type who may ask to be *excused for* responsibilities. I don't want to *save* my *face* for my own mistakes. When I tell you everything *on the face of it* you will easily know what is the truth. My statements will be *far from* untruth. I don't *fear* to tell you the truth for I am *far off* from showy business.

Master : All right. Tell me soon what happened! So far your statements are *far from* point. You are just *beating about the bush* and not coming to the point. *Finish* it all soon before my patience exhausts. Please don't hide anything *for fear of* punishment. I may *excuse* you if you don't *fall short* of my expectation.

**24**

Master : Will you learn to run the car in a proper *gear*? You should not drive it on a *low gear* when there is elevation on the road.

Driver : Yes Master, I shall do so. But I was about to put it in a *high gear* when you asked me to do so.

Master : Better talk less than do it. Or you *get down* and *get away*. People like you who don't *care for* the Master's instructions, don't *go very far*. I would advise you to better *go along with* the instructions.

Driver : Sir, I am *holding* my *breath* to listen to your instructions. I shall *hold on* what you have said right now.

Master : Can you stop the car for a minute near the oncoming gas station (petrol pump) as I want to *inquire about* how far Mumbai is from here?

Driver : Yes sir. I can also *inquire* it if you like.

Master : No, you don't. Better let me *inquire* first. You don't know what to *ask for*. I just want to *inquire* how long traffic has been *held up* before we enter the town.

## 25

*A scene from a one - act play*

A man and a woman named Pradeep and Leela enter the stage from opposite directions and start chatting casually.

Pradeep : Hi Leela! How are you?

Leela : Pradeep, I am seeing you after a long time. Did you go to Mumbai to *join* your family? Or did you utilise your time to *join hands* with any new partners in business?

Pradeep : No, I was here only but I have *joined in* a new club where I pass most of my time in the evening.

Leela : I am sure you are *keeping away* from bad company. Better *keep off* such people who may *let you down* and ruin your career eventually.

A third person named Harry enters the stage suddenly from the western side and addressing Leela says:

Harry : Leela, I advise you to *keep off* Pradeep. Don't *keep him down* with your spells of your beauty. Better *keep* yourself *off* him and let him live his own way. You always try to *knock* good people *down* for nothing (for no reason). Your way of life is so nasty that you try to *kick* a man at his *back* and *knock* him *down* when he needs your help most. I implore you to *lay* your hands *off* Pradeep.

Leela : *Knock down* your anger, Harry. I have done nothing to Pradeep except that I have offered him a bit of advice. Now I ask you to *lay* him *off* for sometime so that he could live in peace. I very much *lay hopes on* Pradeep, as he is one of my best friends.

Listening to that Harry moves away and both, Pradeep and Leela, joining hands together *kick out* the stage.

**26**

Ashok : What makes you *leave* so soon? Did you finish all the work assigned to you? You should be *leaving* only when you have handed over the work to me after you have finished it.

Ramu : Sir, I have done all what you had asked me to do. I am *leaving* a bit earlier today as I have to *leave for* Delhi early tomorrow.

Ashok : Well, let me see what have you done so far. *Leave me alone* after you have handed over the assignment to me.

Ramu : Very well sir, This is the work you had asked me to do. It is complete in all respects. Can I *leave* now?

Ashok : Yes, you can. But can you not *leave over* your Delhi trip for the next week? It will help us in many ways. It will help you not *to leave your work behind* as tomorrow there would be a lot of new assignments.

Ramu : I am not sure to *abandon* my trip to Delhi, but I shall *think it over* again.

**27**

Jeevan : Namrata, what is going on right now? You seem to be pretty busy with you marriage. How is the boy? What has he been doing? Did your parents *let* you see him before marriage?

Namrata : Good morning, uncle. Yes, I am very busy with my marriage preparations. My parents are kind and good. They did *let* me see him a few days before arranging this marriage. In fact, my parents are quite liberal in such matters. They believe in *live and let live*. Besides, as my parents' happiness depends on this marriage, I also thought to *let it go* the way the parents want it to be. The truth is that I am also quite happy with this marriage.

Jeevan : Well, it's a good news. I pray all should go well with you after the marriage. Please *take care* of your valuables. *Lock* your jewellery *in* before you leave this room. Always *lock it up* at your in-laws too when you intend to go out even for a short time.

Namrata : Yes uncle, I shall do as you have advised. *Look* there. Who is coming to see you? She is my aunt. She wants to *look at* the stuff my parents have bought for me. Oh! She *looks good.* Uncle, I have seen you today after a long time. You too *look good.* I pray that you always stay well and good.

Jeevan : Thank you Namrata. Now I *leave.* God bless you.

**28**

Jitendra : I can't believe it that you will *lose* your job so early. What made you *lose* it? You must *look about* a good job in the newspapers. Please *look through* the Ads in most of the leading papers of the country. I am pretty sure you are *going to* get one soon.

Deepak : Yes Jitendra, I shall *look after* it quite seriously as I am without a job right now.

Jitendra : Please don't *lose heart* as you are a qualified person. Soon you will get a job. Never *lose sight* to *look through* the Ads in the newspapers. I pray you get a good position in a week's time only.

Deepak : I appreciate your kind concern and thank you for visiting me. I shall always *keep on the track* and will never *lose sight* until I get a good position.

**29**

Kewal : Pushpa, can you *make* a cup of tea for me? Please *make it with* the dairy milk and not with the powder milk.

Pushpa : Yes my dear, I shall *make it with* the dairy milk but it does not *make* much *sense.* Do you think that dairy milk is better than powder milk?

Kewal : Well, as far as I know dairy milk is surely better than the other one. Have you never *observed* it before? I shall always *pass* dairy milk as the best milk. Please always *keep it with* you and never *part with* it. Dairy milk *pays back* in its own way. It keeps you intact healthwise. So what you *pay out* for it is worth *paying.*

Pushpa : I got you now and understand it why do you *insist upon* using dairy milk in your tea. I never *thought about* it in that way. I simply used any milk to *make* tea. Now, whenever I go *for shopping,* I shall always *pick up* the right kind of milk and will not *pay* any *attention* to any other sort of milk.

Kewal : Please don't misunderstand me. Powder milk has its own merits too but dairy milk *makes* good tea as well as it is more healthy. So I prefer it in tea.

**30**

Raheem : Did you bring my stuff from the shop or you forgot to *pick it up*? Did you pay for it or *made* only a part of the payment against it?

Shameem : I have collected your stuff but haven't paid anything. I thought you must have *paid for* it. I would not have *picked it up* if I knew that I had to *pay* for it. Why do you *play with* me? How would I know that the stuff I had to *pick off* required to be *paid off*? You should have *paid off* for it before asking me to *pick it up*.

Raheem : I am sorry for that. I did not mean to hurt you. Nor I am *playing with* you. As I was talking with a friend when I bought all that, it *slipped off* my mind to *pay for it*. I also forgot to collect it and *walked away* without taking it. The shopkeeper, being a known person, did not even remind me to collect the stuff.

Shameem : Oh! So you are at times so forgetful about your own things. You could have gone back to collect the stuff rather than asking me to *pick it up.* You *pressed me for* it repeatedly but you did not mention that you forgot to *pay for it.*

Raheem : Well Shameem, it is not such a serious matter as you are taking it. I really did not *press* you *for* it. Neither I was *playing with* you about it. It is such a trivial matter that you should forget it. In case you feel hurt, I feel sorry for it.

Shameem : That's allright. Please don't repeat it again in future.

## 31

Badrinarayan : Hay! Why are you *pulling* that chair? If you wish to sit on it in the garden then don't *pull it about. Pull it together* with that small table as well so that we can also use it whenever we require. Better *pull it* gently and don't *pull it apart* by *pulling* it so hard.

Deepak : Yes, *Dada Ji.* I shall *pull* it gently now. But the chair is so heavy that as I am *pulling it through* the living room, I feel as if I am *pulling it off.* But I shall surely *pull through* it into the garden. Oh! Now it is *pulling up* nicely.

Badrinarayan : That's like my grandson. Well done. Will you please *pull* another chair into the garden from the living-room so that two persons can sit in the garden? Please *put away* that dustbin at the right place. Did you notice how those trees in our garden have *put forth* the new leaves? Listen Deepak! Can you *put* these chairs *back* after it is dark and *put out* the light in the garden? You should also *put* the light *on* in the porch.

Deepak : Yes sir. I shall do all that.

**32**

Harish : Have you prepared your speech well so that you may *put it across* the people, who come to listen to you? Use simple words so that it is *within their reach.* Remember one more thing. In case, people *reach out* their hands to meet yours, extend yours too. I *reckon* there will be a good gathering today. I also *reckon in* that at least four to five VIPs will also *join in* to listen to your speech. All the best to you!

Neeta : Thank you sir. I am trying my best to improve my speech. I hope I shall *reckon with* my speech well. I am hoping *to make* it so interesting that none *retires* before I conclude it. I shall *reckon in* every important detail of the government expenditure on the new settlers. It shall *make* my speech really interesting and will *make* the VIPs *stay* there longer.

Harish : Well *thought of* plan. Please don't *reflect* any figures in the speech that are *beyond the reach* of the ordinary public. There will be a lot of *retired* persons in the gathering too. Don't forget to *reflect* some gestures to fascinate every kind of person, lest some of them should *retire into* themselves.

Neeta : I appreciate your valuable advice. I shall *round up* my speech keeping in view all what you have said right now. I really want to *ride on* well and don't wish to *ride for a fall.* Harish, will you please run across my cousin's place to borrow a fan from him? I need it badly. The time is *running against* me. I need to be *ready to* go to the office. I have also *run out* some grocery. Would you wind the clock on the wall? It seems to have *run down*. I *reckon* I am trying to *run after* the time to do everything well. Oh, it is so exciting to prepare a good speech. I shall try to *save* sometime from my office routine to prepare myself *to face* the VIPs. Is it not a challenge to be *face to face* with such big people, especially when you are the main speaker in a gathering?

Harish : Oh yes, it is true. You are so lucky to be invited as the principal speaker in that gathering where a good number of VIPs are also invited to attend.

Good luck to you, Neeta.

Neeta : Thank you, Harish. Please don't forget to *run across* my cousin to ask for a fan.

Harish : No, I wouldn't.

**33**

Prakash : Did you hear about Satish's accident? He was badly injured but *saved* by a good doctor who lives just nearby.

Mohan : How did the accident happen? How much was Satish hurt? Please tell me all in detail. Do you know that Satish is one of my good friends? I am really obliged to the doctor who *saved* him *from* dying.

Prakash : It happened so that when Satish was driving through the hospital road on Monday morning, a motorcyclist ran into his car and damaged his back door badly. The one who was driving the motorcycle was a young boy, who did not understand the dangers of running so fast on a crowded road. The boy lost his balance when the car reached nearer. Not only the back door was badly damaged, he also hit Satish from his right side. Satish sustained some injuries, which could be fatal. But thank God. He was *saved* by that doctor. The accident cost Satish a lot. I *reckon* we all should *save up* for future for such unforeseen happenings.

Mohan : Prakash, I am so surprised with how people behave on the road. If a vehicle is moving in their direction just in front of them they don't *get away* or *stand aside*. They will go on standing right there. They will never *stand back* or even try to *move* a bit on the other side. I think all this should be taught in schools to enlighten the children and to help them *save* themselves from the road hazards.

**34**

Zameel : The workers seem to be on *strike* today as none is in their seats though it is eleven o'clock in the morning. What has happened? Why are they not in their seats? If they don't *turn in* by tomorrow, the Managing Director may *strike off* their names from the rolls. An idea has just *struck on* in my mind. Why should we not call a meeting of the workers to know their grievances? Let us try to solve their problems as far as possible. These are very hard times. If anyone of them is *laid off,* he will be a great sufferer. Once if the MD *strikes off* someone's name from the job, he cannot be *taken back.*

Amit : Yes, you are right. The new MD is very strict. He will never *take into account* anyone's request after he is removed from the job. You can *take it down* that the MD rules by the law. He will never *take* his orders *back.* So the workers must *take upon* them for every action they do in this office.

Zameel : You are right, Amit. I haven't seen such a strict person in my life. He is also very punctual. He will always *take off* at the right time and will enter the office just *on time.* I *reckon* he has *taken to* such habits in the company of his seniors. Besides, as soon as he enters the office, he *strikes up* his work and continues until it is 5 P.M. I really have a lot of respect for him. In this office, there are not many senior people, who really are so punctual and serious about work.

Amit : Yes, you are right, Zameel. I think we all should learn from such people, and do a good job for our company. But let us first solve the problem of the workers. Please arrange to call a meeting of the workers along with the Managing Director. But before that we must *take into confidence* all the workers so that they behave properly in front of the MD.

Zameel : Yes, you are right. Let us inform all the workers to meet in the office before 10 A.M to discuss their problems.

**35**

Mohan : Laloo, did you see that the living room is so dirty that none can even *stand* in it for a minute? As soon as I entered into it, I had to *step aside* as it was smelling so badly. Look at the windowpanes! They are absolutely dirty and need to be *scraped* at once. Call the maid to *scrape* grease and dirt *from* the windows and the doors. Let her *scrape out* dirt and grease from the floor as well as it is also very dirty. Hay! Look at the curtains! It seems someone has *wiped* dirty hands *with* them. Try to *search* who could be the one to wipe hands with the curtains?

Laloo : Yes sir, I shall *search for* it. I shall also try to *search for* one who wiped dirty hands with the curtains. I *reckon* it could be children who would have done so. *See*, there are also some dirt marks on the walls. I can *see* clearly some small hands' marks there. I am sure these are the children who have done all that mischief.

Mohan : Call the children and *inquire of* them whether they did all that. *(Children are asked to come before Mohan)*. Who will tell me who did all that? *(They stand quietly before him with bend heads.)*

Laloo : Sir, I know they have done all that mischief so they are quiet. Please let them go. I shall manage to clean everything well with the help of the maid.

Mohan : Allright! If you say so, I shall let them go this time but next time if anything of that nature happens I shall *see them off* and keep them in a hostel. Laloo, please *search for* each spot where dirty marks are there and get them cleaned very properly. Please *see about* every dirty place and *see back* the maid when she is working to clean the room. *Send for* the other maid too to help you in this venture. I advise you to *sell off* all the useless stuff of this room and *send away* the other maid when you think the work is finished.

Laloo : I know what you mean. I shall *see* that everything is done well. I shall *see across* the room before dismissing the maids that it is absolutely cleaned. I shall *take care* that every article, chairs and sofa are *set in* at its place and the room *looks good.*

Mohan : Thank you, Laloo. I hope you will do what I have said and *take care* of the children too for they are innocent and don't know what they have done to this room. One more thing to remember. Please don't forget to *sell up* the unwanted stuff and *pay off* the dues of the grocery shop with it.

Laloo : I shall do that also. You be *rest assured* I shall *take care of* all what you have said. Please go to the office with a cheerful mood. Nothing will be *left out* to *set* this room *well.*

**36**

Ashutosh : Did you *send* the messenger to fetch the mail and post it in time? At times, it is necessary to *send away* the messenger not only to post or collect letters but also to buy things that we don't get in this small place. Tell me how is this new messenger? Is his work good or he also needs to be *sent down* like the former one? Please *send for* him right now as I have some other work for him. *(The new messenger named Harry is asked to come)*

Harry : Sir, did you *send for* me? By the way, I have posted all the letters and also collected the mail from the post office. You asked me to buy some grocery from the supermarket. I have bought most of the stuff but some of the articles were not available in the shop. I could not buy them. I have also *sent out* the gifts to the respective persons as you had desired.

Ashutosh : Very well. I am glad that you *took care* for my orders. If you will *serve* us well, we shall award you well too. A few years ago when I was working in the university, I *served on* in various committees. Luckily, we had a good servant working for us in one of the committees. He *served* us *out* so well that I still remember him. He was very obedient and intelligent as well. He *served out* all equally well. I want you to be like him, Harry.

Harry : I shall try to be like him, Sir. I know how to *serve for*. The only thing I want is to *settle down* well in this house. Once if I am *settled well* after *settling with* you, you will never have any complaint against me.

Ashutosh : What sort of *settlement* do you want *with* us? I have already told you our terms and conditions. I shall always *abide by* those terms and *settle with* you as *agreed upon.* You simply need to *shake down* here for it is absolutely a new environment for you. Never get depressed on any account and try to *shake off* on account of work. Try to be satisfied with what has been *settled on* and don't try to *shake off* from here.

Harry : Well said sir. I am not a fugitive who runs away with the pressure of the problems. I know how to fight the adverse circumstances and take them *face to face* when need arises. None can *shake* me *out,* as I am so strong within. Besides, I always *set forth* on a new venture with great determination and never *lose courage* in odd circumstances. I am accustomed to hardships. Since my childhood, I had to *work for* my living. I shall never *tear away* on account of impediments. I never like to be *torn between* any diverse situations as I know which way, I should follow.

Ashutosh : Well said Harry. I like your comments and way of thinking. Someone like you would never stop from going high. I am afraid you will be doing a small job at our place. Your experience and qualification are far better than the job, you will do here. But

I like you and wish to retain you as far as I can. If you *serve* us *well*, you will equally be rewarded for your services. You seem to be an honest person too. I shall think to provide you a good accommodation in our back quarters.

Harry : I am sincerely thankful to you sir for your kind gesture and generosity.

**37**

Shopkeeper : What do you want to buy today? I think I have most of the things you require for your household.

Customer : Do you have sugar and cereals as well as some fresh vegetables?

Shopkeeper : I have told you I have everything that you need for your kitchen and house as well. I also *sell* things cheaper than the other shopkeepers, as I buy things in bulk from distant towns and cities just to *keep* the price *down* keeping in view my customers' interest.

Customer : Can you provide me the list of articles along with their prices so that I could compare the prices and know what things are there in the shop?

Shopkeeper : Here it is sir. There are a few more things that I also *sell*. Many of those are not listed here in. I am prepared to *sell* them *to* you whenever you are ready to buy them. I have a telephone too. If you like you can *send away* from home on phone and I shall arrange to *send* things to you at once.

Customer : You seem to be a nice shopkeeper. Do you also have some sorts of juices? I like to drink a glass of juice.

Shopkeeper : Oh yes! I have pineapple and orange juice with me. Would you care to drink some juice right now? *(The customer nods to get one.)* Here it is. Please *shake* the bottle well before you drink it. If you think you like the juice, you can *tear off* the label from the bottle to remember the name of the company, it made.

Customer : Oh, it tastes good. I *think* the company that made it is good. Let me *tear off* its tag to remember its name to *send away* for some of these things from home. But I shall *think about* to buy vegetables from your shop, as they don't *look* as fresh as I had *thought*.

Shopkeeper : Sir, you may *think it out* to reject my vegetables. They are *not only* fresh *but also* cheaper in comparison to other places.

Customer : Allright. I shall *think of* it before ordering. I shall also *think over* to visit you next week *in case* you bring some new stuff and fresher vegetables.

**38**

Sheela : I have learnt that you are *thinking* to buy a new house, Anurag.

Anurag : Yes, you are right. I am *thinking it out* to buy a new house. It is situated in a good locality. Could you please *think over* about my plan to buying that house. If you were in my position how would you have reacted upon my plan?

Sheela : I *reckon* your plan to buy that house is good, but after taking a decision, please don't try to *throw it off*, if you find it later on less suitable. Therefore, *think about* it from every angle before buying it.

Anurag : I have *thought it over* from every side and feel that it will be good to buy it. Actually, I am not *throwing myself at* the idea of buying the house, but to shift to that house will be beneficial to us in many ways. First of all, I feel to be *tied down* in this house, we are living right now, as there is no room for the children to play. I am also *tired out* here as the main market is pretty far away from here. Considering all that my plan seems to be worthwhile.

Sheela : *Go ahead* then. Don't delay to buy it lest someone else should buy it. *If I were you*, I would have paid for it as soon as I could. I have seen that house, a few months back. I feel you would need to *touch it up* at certain places before occupying it. But you will know where you really require *touching up* only when you start living in it.

Anurag : Yes, you are right. So you also approve of my decision. I shall act upon it as soon as I can. Thank you, Sheela for your advice and good thinking.

## 39

Seema : Shyam, where are you going so early? Please *wait for* me for a few minutes. I am also getting ready to *move out* for some important work. Will you please give me lift unto the main market so that I could buy some foodstuff for the house?

Shyam : Yes I can *wait for* you for sometime but not endlessly. Please don't make me *wait up* for you for an hour as you are *wont to* do. Why do you want me to *wait on* you everyday? You must realise that you waste a lot of my time *waiting on* you for hours before I go to office.

Seema : You are not right. It would have hardly happened only two or three times in a year when I asked you to wait for me. I don't make you *wait on* me for hours. It is you who often get late for your office because you get up so late in the morning.

Shyam : It is not true. I am hardly late for the office. If I am late, it is *because of* you. You often make me *wait up* in the night for flimsy reasons. It is because I sleep late that I wake up late. Seema, you have a good art to *turn about* the way you like. When I point out that you make me late to go to office, you just start blaming me.

Seema : Now onwards, you will never be late *on account of* me. I will sleep in the other room from tonight and will never give you a chance to *wait on* me. Besides, it will also help me to read a lot before I sleep. It is because of you that I have to sleep early as you want the light to be *turned out.* Now, please go ahead. I am not going to the market with you.

Shyam : Don't get annoyed for no reason. I am *waiting for* you to take you to the market. But please hurry up and get ready soon.

Seema : I can come with you only on one condition. It is that you would not press me to be ready so hastily. By now, you should have learnt that ladies take little more time in getting ready.

Shyam : Allright. Now it is already so late for the office. I am really *tired of* your getting ready so leisurely. Please *turn aside* your anger and get ready soon if you want to go with me.

**40**

Rohitash : It is quite late now. Let us *walk* briskly back home. Where are the other girls? Ask them to follow us. Our house is pretty far away from here. It will take us at least twenty minutes to reach home.

Nirmala : Some of them are very tired, so they cannot walk fast. Did you notice, Rohitash how some of them *walked into* the rice pudding in the restaurant? Perhaps, they were very hungry, or they liked the sweet so much that they never seemed to be *stopping* when once started eating it.

Rohitash : It was a strange sight to see the girls eating. Some of them did not even *wipe* their hands and ate in a great hurry. You can see a few stains of food on their dresses. It reflects their bad manners as well as makes me think that they were so hungry that they did not care for their clothes and ate so hurriedly. Is it possible to *wipe away* the stains from their dresses?

Nirmala : I am sure a good detergent can *wipe off* most of the stains. The greasy spots can also be *wiped up* by *rubbing* them *off* with a good washing soap.

Rohitash : It seems that a storm is awaiting all of us. Let us hurry back home so that we reach safely and the girls, who seem to be sleepy now, can have a good night's rest to start afresh for tomorrow.

# Exercises

***A. Choose one of the correct idioms or phrases to fit into the following sentences out of the alternatives given below each sentence. The incorrect phrase or idiom is underlined in each sentence.***

1. She looked back on him instantly.
   (a) looked back against
   (b) looked back on
   (c) looked back with
   (d) looked back into
   (e) looked back at

   Answer: (e) *looked at angrily*

2. He lost his sight of the right path on account of darkness.
   (a) lost his eyes
   (b) lost his track
   (c) lost his light
   (d) lost sight
   (e) lost his sight

   Answer: (d) *failed to take account*

3. If you like you can make in anything from this document.
   (a) can make for
   (b) can make out
   (c) can make in
   (d) can make with
   (e) can make sense

Answer: (b) *to deduce*

4. He passed away around 4 P. M. yesterday.
   (a) passed with
   (b) passed in
   (c) passed away
   (d) passed out
   (e) passed off

Answer: (d) *died*

5. She often picks up good flowers from the vendor while returning from her job.
   (a) picks out
   (b) picks on
   (c) picks over
   (d) picks at
   (e) picks off

Answer: (a) *to choose or distinguish*

6. They are likely to reckon on the dealer after sometime when the dust is settled.
   (a) reckon in

(b) reckon with
(c) reckon upon
(d) reckon up
(e) reckon on

Answer: (b) *deal with*

7. After his retirement, he has retired from himself.
   (a) retired from
   (b) retired with
   (c) retired to
   (d) retired for
   (e) retired into

Answer: (e) *withdrawn from social life*

8. You seem to have run after a lot in a month's time.
   (a) run against
   (b) run along
   (c) run down
   (d) run away
   (e) run into

Answer: (c) *become weak or exhausted*

9. We all must save in some provisions for tomorrow.
   (a) save in
   (b) save from
   (c) save up
   (d) save out
   (e) save against

Answer: (c) *to keep for future*

10. Our new boss is a good person. He always stands for all.

(a) stands in
(b) stands up
(c) stands with
(d) stands by
(e) stands for

Answer: (c) *to be in good terms with*

11. When Ramesh and his father stand side by side, they both take up each other.

(a) take with
(b) take after
(c) take in
(d) take up
(e) take to

Answer: (b) *to resemble in features*

12. Both the sons are so cruel that they turned down their father in the world.

(a) turned about
(b) turned adrift
(c) turned aside
(d) turned away
(e) turned down

Answer: (b) *sent away without support*

13. The plane touched in the ground around at 5 o' clock in the evening.

(a) touched at
(b) touched in
(c) touched down
(d) touched on
(e) touched up

Answer: (c) *came down to land*

14. As soon as they returned from the picnic, they settled up their beds immediately.

(a) settled in
(b) settled up
(c) settled down
(d) settled into
(e) settled for

Answer: (c) *sat or lied comfortably*

15. As soon as she entered the restaurant, she walked on to the sweets.

(a) walked into
(b) walked for
(c) walked to
(d) walked in
(e) walked about

Answer: (a) *ate heartily*

***B. Following set of exercises contain sentences in which the underlined words require to be replaced by one of the correct idioms or phrases given after each sentence. Answers are provided at the end of these exercises.***

1. He declined to continue working as the President of the Society further.
   (a) backed up
   (b) backed out
   (c) backed in
   (d) backed for
   (e) backed into

2. Let the students sometimes release their tension to help them work smoothly.
   (a) blow off
   (b) blow out
   (c) blow over
   (d) blow in
   (e) blow up

3. Our Prime Minister is very open and is without any deception.
   (a) boarding
   (b) board in
   (c) across the board
   (d) above board
   (e) board and bold

4. The thief made his way through the locked house and stole valuables worth hundreds of thousand rupees.
   (a) broke in
   (b) broke off
   (c) broke out
   (d) broke into
   (e) broke through

5. When I looked at the photograph of my father, it recalled many of his great deeds.
   (a) carried back
   (b) carried in
   (c) carried away
   (d) carried for
   (e) carried forward

6. She has abandoned the traditional way of her living and adopted new ones.
   (a) changed in
   (b) changed over
   (c) changed to
   (d) changed for
   (e) changed from

7. The thief obstinately resisted to reveal anything when forced by the police.
   (a) died away
   (b) died from
   (c) died for

(d) died hard
(e) died in

8. She <u>did not take</u> her final examination on account of her illness.
   (a) dropped out
   (b) dropped in
   (c) dropped into
   (d) dropped at
   (e) dropped off

9. He was <u>permitted not to attend</u> his hospital duties to help his ailing mother.
   (a) excused for
   (b) excused from
   (c) excused by
   (d) excused in
   (e) excused of

10. The expenses of her father's illness <u>became her responsibility by chance</u>.
    (a) fell on
    (b) fell into
    (c) fell in
    (d) fell out
    (e) fell over

11. I can easily <u>manage with</u> my new principal.
    (a) get down

(b) get along
(c) get out
(d) get about
(e) get away

12. We were <u>delayed</u> at the railway station for a couple of hours as the train arrived late.
    (a) held up
    (b) held down
    (c) held breath
    (d) held out
    (e) held on

13. We tried to <u>walk and go forward</u> with others with the same pace.
    (a) keep out
    (b) keep away
    (c) keep back
    (d) keep up
    (e) keep in

14. The police <u>chased</u> the thief and finally caught him near the main market.
    (a) made in
    (b) made after
    (c) made out
    (d) made away
    (e) made over

15. The owner of the factory expelled a few workers from the factory last night.
    (a) laid over
    (b) laid out
    (c) laid in
    (d) laid off
    (e) laid aside

16. We carefully examined and made selection of a basket full of apples.
    (a) picked in
    (b) picked over
    (c) picked out
    (d) picked up
    (e) picked off

17. Please don't intervene in my matters, as I am capable enough to take care of myself.
    (a) step off
    (b) step out
    (c) step up
    (d) step in
    (e) step aside

18. The Water Works Department has stopped the supply of water for two days.
    (a) shut out
    (b) shut off

(c) shut in
(d) shut up
(e) shut down

19. Sania Mirza won easily in the Tennis finals in London.
(a) walked away
(b) walked off
(c) walked into
(d) walked out
(e) walked away with

20. They fastened the banner with the strings on the post.
(a) tie it up
(b) tied it down
(c) tied it for
(d) tied it on
(e) tied it upon

***Answers:*** 1. (b), 2. (a), 3. (d) 4. (e), 5. (a), 6. (b), 7. (d), 8. (a), 9. (b), 10. (a), 11. (b), 12. (a), 13. (d), 14. (b), 15. (b), 16. (b), 17. (d), 18. (b), 19. (e), 20. (d)

## C. Sentence Correction

***A part of a sentence or the entire sentence is underlined in each of the following sentences. Five alternatives are given beneath each sentence to replace the underlined part. You may choose the best alternative out of the five. These exercises are simply given to help you know more about common mistakes that one often commits, while writing or speaking English.***

1. The main reason of their failing was quite evident to those whom they had brought into the adventure.
   (a) to those whom they had brought
   (b) to them whom they had brought
   (c) to the ones whom they had brought
   (d) to those who they had brought
   (e) to those who they had brought

   Answer: (a) *No error*

2. He is the kind of person who I think would be capable of making these kind of remarks.
   (a) who I think would be capable of making these kind of
   (b) who I think would be capable of making these kinds of
   (c) who I think would be capable of making this kind of
   (d) whom I think would be capable of making these kinds of

(e) whom I think would be capable of making this kind of

Answer: (b)

3. He rose to state that in his opinion, he thought, the rule should be referred back to the President for amendment.

   (a) in his opinion he thought the rule should be referred back
   (b) he thought the rule should be referred back
   (c) he thought that it must be referred back
   (d) in his opinion the rule should be referred
   (e) he thought the rule should be referred

Answer: (e) words *in his opinion* & *back* are not required.

4. Whoever objects to him going to the theatre should say it immediately.

   (a) objects to him going to
   (b) objects to me going to
   (c) objects to him going to
   (d) objects to his going to
   (e) objects to he going to

Answer: (d) the correct use of the pronoun is *his* and not him

5. Deepak, the secretary of the company and who is also a member of the finance committee, will accompany the foreign dignitary.

(a) who is also a member of the finance committee
(b) who is as well as a member of the finance committee
(c) since he is a member of the finance committee
(d) a member of the finance committee
(e) who is a member of the finance committee as well

Answer: (d) words like '*who is also,*' are superfluous.

6. Because they cooperated with one another, they divided up the work, which had been assigned.
   (a) with one another, they divided up the work on the report which had been assigned
   (b) with one another, they divided the work on the report which had been assigned
   (c) they divided up the work on the report which was assigned
   (d) they divided the work on the assigned report
   (e) they divided up the work on the assigned report

   Answer: (d) *It's a precise and to the point expression.*

7. On account of continual wind, the clouds scattered and it resulted that it did not rain.
   (a) As the wind continued, the clouds scattered which resulted in no rains.
   (b) It did not rain because the clouds scattered on account of continued wind.
   (c) On account of continual wind, the clouds got scattered and it stopped raining.
   (d) On account of continued wind, the clouds scattered and resulted in not raining.

(e) As the wind continued and the clouds scattered as a consequence it stopped raining.

Answer: (b) *it seems to be* the most befitting expression.

8. Besides me, there were many people, who did not approve of his odd mannerism.
   (a) There were many people besides me, who did not approve of his odd mannerism.
   (b) Besides me, who did not approve of his odd mannerism, there were many people.
   (c) Besides many people I was also there who did not approve of his odd mannerism.
   (d) Many people as well as me were there who did not approve of his odd mannerism.
   (e) Besides many people, me was also there who did not approve of his odd mannerism.

Answer: (a) *It's a most precise* and to the point *expression.*

9. The car, driven by an experienced driver with an outdated engine, must be sent to the junkyard.
   (a) driven by an experienced driver must be sent to the junkyard with an outdated engine.
   (b) driven by an experienced driver, with an outdated engine, must be sent to the junkyard.
   (c) with an outdated engine driven by an experienced driver, must be sent to the junkyard.
   (d) having an outdated engine and driven by an experienced driver must be sent to the junk yard.

(e) fitted with an outdated engine though driven by an experienced driver must be sent to the junkyard.

Answer: (b) *two commas put after* driver and engine provide better sense.

10. Having managed her home for many years, she understood her family better.

(a) Because she managed her home for years she understood her family better.

(b) As she managed her home for many years, she understood her family better.

(c) Having managed her home for many years she could understand her family better.

(d) For many years she managed her home, so she understood her family better.

(e) Managing her home for many years she was able to understand her family better.

Answer: (b) *It provides the best meaning* and sense. Normally, we don't *start a sentence with* because.

11. Since we were living in Delhi for many years we were reluctant to move to a smaller city.

(a) As we were living in Delhi for many years we were reluctant to move to a smaller city.

(b) Since we lived in Delhi for many years we were reluctant to move to a smaller city.

(c) As for many years we lived in Delhi, we were reluctant to move to a smaller city.

(d) Since we had been living in Delhi for many years, we were reluctant to move to a smaller city.

(e) We lived in Delhi for many years we were reluctant to move to a smaller city.

Answer: (d) *Past perfect tense is* correct in this case.

12. The teacher, who was very kind spoke to the student and he was very rude.

(a) who was very kind he spoke to the student who

(b) was a kind person and he spoke to the student who

(c) spoke to the student kindly and the student

(d) a kind person, spoke to the student who

(e) who was a kind person spoke to the student and he

Answer: (d) *It's a more precise and to the point expression.*

13. Peter had never done it if he would have known that it would hurt his parents.

(a) would have never done it if he had

(b) had done it never if he would have

(c) would have not have done it if he had

(d) would never do it if he would have

(e) had never done it if he had

Answer: (a) *It makes the sentence past* conditional, which is the correct usage in this case.

14. Any one desirous to get admission in the college should submit their applications before the closing date, which is July $15^{th}$.

(a) submit their application
(b) submit her application
(c) submit their applications in
(d) submit an application
(e) submit their application in

Answer: (d) *As anyone is singular, it will not take 'their' application.*

15. A good teacher not only needs to know the students thoroughly, but requires to know their parents well.

(a) but requires to find out
(b) but needs to find out
(c) but also requires to know
(d) but requires to see
(e) but requires to meet

Answer: (c) *'not only' is followed by 'but also'.*